Let's Talk Social Equality:
Race and Religion
in Politics

By

Raffi E. Andonian

7/2020

to Steve,

Best wishes

in Rotary service,

Raffi Andonian

First Printing: 2020

ISBN: 978-0-9963197-8-2

Cronus Media Ventures, LLC
Columbus, Ohio

Epoch Publishing
San Diego, CA

www.CronusMediaVentures.com

www.RaffiAndonian.com

TABLE OF CONTENTS

Publisher's Note

When writing about historical events, it is sometimes difficult to find a balance between readability and preservation of items like vernacular and original language usage. Out of respect for the past, we have kept direct quotations and referenced documents in their original form. Some words may seem misspelled and some phrasing unfamiliar, but this is primarily since the word usage has changed over the centuries. In several "extreme" cases, we opted to use a more modern word or spelling to add clarity when the original form was too unrecognizable.

Introduction: A Case for Complexity and Dialogue

A historical understanding of race is the only way we can fully understand racial issues in our contemporary society. Each aspect of this issue has a past that has led to current outcomes. Understanding the origins, developments since, and the people and forces that shaped it into present circumstances helps us decipher what we are seeing and how to make the changes appropriate to solving these problems. It may be tempting and common to select bits from the past to reinforce what we already believe about today. Still, when we remove ourselves from our predetermined conclusion, we discover a past far more complex than anticipated – and therefore equally complicated answers.

Similarly, the boundaries of the freedom of religion have been defined and redefined for generations. We tend to assert that which makes the most sense from our position of faith to simplify our perceptions of the problem and the solution. While a member of a particular spiritual community, or lack thereof, may view the past through their specific lens of beliefs, definitions of these boundaries have been debated and changed over time, even by the founders and thought leaders of this principle that has been codified into United States law and mores. There is no single truth in the answer, because even the foundational documents and people for whom we hold this principle so dear, did not view this matter in a simple way. It was complicated for them then and will always remain so, for us today and into the future.

Perhaps instead of jumping to answers, we should be asking more questions. Crusades to prove a point do not lead to the appropriate framing of inquiry, or an honest answer. The study of history remains vibrant because it is driven by fresh questions from each scholar and each generation, all offering a new perspective. Stepping back from the passion of one's position to inquire with fresh eyes, even the eyes, such as empathy, with whom we may disagree, might lead us to more nuanced views based on recognizing the complexity of the past, which is captured in the present issue, to lead us to integrated societal solutions. Otherwise, we are caught in the arm-wrestling of factions, winners and losers, doing and undoing – without any sustainable outcomes to move forward constructively.

This collection of essays aims to surprise us. It is neither Left nor Right, because the past doesn't know how to fit neatly into one political camp. People of the past cannot be placed into a modern political paradigm, nor can issues with so many layers that extend still further beyond what these essays cover. Reading this book will provoke the reader into more profound reflection, challenging assumptions, and raising questions. The realization that there is more to know is more powerful than the sense of definitive conclusions and entrenched positions. We must not close the book regarding our understanding of these issues; we must all open the book anew.

The essays surprise the reader as follows:

1. In reading about the American view of Haiti in its early decades, we see an argument made for racial equality, yet the basis for making this case derives from a buy-in by black American leaders into Euro-centric definitions of civilization and the accompanying racial notions. The identity of the

advocate becomes irrelevant when such ubiquitous notions permeate across color lines to shape views of racial hierarchies.

2. What is social equality? The Knights of Labor tried to avoid "social equality" while uniting across black and white to have solidarity in labor. In its peak, a specific incident caused a national debate about what they stand for. The Knights and most of its supporters did not view coming together in labor as practicing "social equality," but the public introduction of a white man by a black man broke an unwritten social code, which triggered a debate on the boundaries of what "social equality" means. For an interracial organization to get caught in such a controversy that helped its demise might be surprising to the reader – and the difficulty in defining what this term means continues today, as a vague collective notion which we each interpret differently and regularly clash.

3. The final essay analyzes the origins of religious freedom in the US, rooted in the Commonwealth of Virginia, and concludes what many modern readers would not expect. Many today conflate religious

freedom with the separation of church and state, and therefore believe that this issue is driven in part by an embrace of scientific reason and a rejection of the church. But those who established the concept and the early laws did not do so as secular thinkers or citizens. Instead, they did so as Christians on behalf of God, protecting the purity of the church, with the state as a potential source of poison. Today this realization challenges both Right and Left, in notions of church and state.

Perhaps no issues related to social equality are more frequently in the headlines and debated than those of race and religion. These essays seek not to provide the last word, but to provoke each of us to a new line of thinking with room for challenging ourselves with further layers of learning that remove us from a clear understanding and a simple position. Indeed, all sides of our political spectrum have elements to contribute; history will not show us who's right, it will complicate our understanding enough to begin listening to each other, researching in good faith together, and constructively creating sustainable solutions.

The Black Republic as a Black Star

African Americans Look to Haiti

Race in Latin America[1] helped define racial identities and politics in the United States. The Haitian Revolution rang loudly throughout the Atlantic world, and even helped reshape it;[2] in the United States, Americans were hostile, but its social and political impact was tremendous.[3]

---

[1] Henry Louis Gates, Jr., *Black in Latin America* (New York: New York University Press, 2011); Nancy Priscilla Naro, *Blacks, Coloureds and National Identity in Nineteenth-Century Latin America* (London: Institute of Latin American Studies, University of London, 2003).

[2] David P. Geggus, ed., *The Impact of the Haitian Revolution in the Atlantic World* (Columbia: University of South Carolina Press, 2001); Martin Munro and Elizabeth Walcott-Hacksaw, eds., *Reinterpreting the Haitian Revolution and Its Cultural Aftershocks* (Kingston: University of West Indies Press, 2006); David Brion Davis, *The Problem of Slavery in the Age of Revolution, 1770-1823* (Ithaca: Cornell University Press, 1975); Winthrop D. Jordan, *White over Black: American Attitudes toward the Negro, 1550-1812* (Chapel Hill: University of North Carolina Press, 1968); Valentina Peguero, "Teaching the Haitian Revolution: Its Place in Western and Modern World History," *The History Teacher*, Vol. 32, No. 1 (Nov. 1998), pp. 33-41.

[3] David Brion Davis, *The Problem of Slavery in the Age of Revolution, 1770-1823* (Ithaca: Cornell University Press, 1975); Winthrop D. Jordan, *White*

With slavery as the glaring shortcoming of the American Revolutionary generation, as even most of the U.S. founders acknowledged and grappled,[4] Haiti posed a tricky puzzle to ponder for this idealistic group with imperfect human shortcomings.[5] They cherished and applauded republicanism; but black people, who they believed to lack self-possession in their extravagant and decadent ways, could not steer republicanism so noble, delicate, righteous, and educated.

---

over Black: American Attitudes toward the Negro, 1550-1812 (Chapel Hill: University of North Carolina Press, 1968).

[4] For the best succinct overview on this much-covered topic outside the scope of this essay, see: William W. Freehling, "The Founding Fathers and Slavery," *The American Historical Review*, Vol. 77, No. 1 (Feb. 1972), pp. 81-93.

[5] Gordon S. Brown, *Toussaint's Clause: The Founding Fathers and the Haitian Revolution* (Jackson: University Press of Mississippi, 2005); Arthur Scherr, *Thomas Jefferson's Haitian Policy: Myths and Realities* (New York: Lexington Books, 2011); Ronald Angelo Johnson, "A Revolutionary Dinner: U.S. Diplomacy toward Saint Domingue, 1798-1801," *Early American Studies: An Interdisciplinary Journal*, Vol. 9, No. 1 (Winter 2011), pp. 114-141; Tim Matthewson, "Jefferson and Haiti," *The Journal of Southern History*, Vol. 61, No. 2 (May 1995), pp. 209.248.

With an image of African Americans at home that portrayed them as unstable, disorderly, and chaotic, with an indulgent unrestrained manner that needed white guidance to avoid excess. White Americans overwhelmingly did not believe that black people abroad could govern a fragile republic. However, these pervasive concepts of enlightened republicanism underlay the efforts by African American leaders, who fervently desired and relentlessly endeavored to identify with Haiti as the ultimate symbol of black capability and proof of the falsehood of white supremacy.

Early during the rebellion on the island, the paradox of widespread white American condemnation was not lost on an atypical white New Englander. Abraham Bishop from Connecticut. He was living in Boston in late 1791, when he published in a local newspaper, *The Argus*, a series of three articles entitled, "The Rights of Black Men."[6] After pointing out that the

---

[6] Abraham Bishop, *The Argus* (Boston), 6 December 1791; reprinted, in full, in Tim Matthewson, "Abraham Bishop,'The Rights of Black Men,' and the American Reaction to the Haitian Revolution," *The Journal of Negro History*, Vol. 67, No. 2 (Summer, 1982), pp. 148-154.

"enlightened mind of Americans" believed that "freedom is the natural rights of all rational beings," Bishop asked about the Haitians, "Is not their cause as just as ours?"[7] They were asserting through violence what was not possible to assert through peaceful measures, and this was not unlike what the United States had done in its own quest for independence, he argued. Therefore, Bishop decisively stated, "Believing our cause to have been just, I believe firmly, that the cause of the Blacks is just."[8] He recalled that in the American Revolution, the "hand of Providence" was said to be at work.[9] Recognizing that the revolution had sparked similar movements in other parts of the world, Bishop asked, "Shall we now cease to glory? Shall we now sacrifice principle to a paltry partiality of colour? We shall now see the hand of Providence more visibly, than ever."[10] He stressed that the common blood all humans share, as a whole under this Almighty: *"The Universal Father seems now demonstrating that of one blood, he has created all nation of men, that dwell on the*

---

[7] Bishop, *The Argus* (Boston), 6 December 1791; reprinted in *The Journal of Negro History*.
[8] Ibid.
[9] Ibid.
[10] Ibid.

face of the earth."[11] Bishop asserted that Americans were "zealous in the *theory* of liberty," but the problem was that "we glory in the equal rights of men, provided that *we white men can enjoy the whole of them.*"[12]

He expressed disappointed, even in the antislavery societies of the United States. These societies were not in support of the Haitian Revolution, they wanted the slaves to have petitioned for freedom rather than taking up arms to fight for it. Bishop wondered how they could suggest such "coolness and moderation," when the Americans themselves went to war with Great Britain for their revolution.[13] In addition, beyond just the hypocrisy, petitioning made no practical sense. He found it unrealistic to believe that petitioning would have convinced the French to give the African slaves their freedom as human beings and their independence as a republic. As Bishop wrote, "If that, which is the right of the blacks cannot be quietly obtained, I wish success to their arms... The sword is drawn, blood must shed, and freedom must be obtained."[14]

---

[11] Ibid.
[12] Ibid.
[13] Ibid.

Bishop claimed that he was arguing for the Haitians' freedom based on some of the most central philosophies found in the U.S. American Revolution from its most defining documents: the petitions that were sent to the English courts during the American Revolution, the Declaration of Independence, and Tom Paine's *Common Sense*. Referring to the famous battle cry of the American Revolution, Bishop reasoned, "Have we already forgotten the animating sound, *Liberty or Death*? That sound has gone out into the world, and is rapidly extending to the end of the earth."[15] However, race stood in the way of acknowledging vindication of these prized values of the American Revolution: "We have firmly asserted, *that all men are free*. The blacks are entitled to freedom, for we did not say, all *white* men are *free*, but *all men* are free."[16]

Bishop believed that it was the duty of America to assist the Haitian revolutionaries, since what they were fighting for was the precise ideology the Americans claimed to cherish, uphold, and promote. "It is cruelty then to withhold such aid and support and worse than

---

[14] Ibid.
[15] Ibid.
[16] Ibid.

cruelty to assist their enemies," Bishop deduced.[17] Americans had indeed sent assistance to the enemies of the black rebels. The George Washington administration, the Pennsylvania legislature and the government of South Carolina had all sent help to the white French of Saint Domingue. Bishop saw only God remaining on the side of the black revolutionaries. He affirmed with hope "He has put it into their hearts to assert their own cause. He is leading them, as he taught you, that freedom from the tyranny of men is to be had *only* at the price of blood. By this lesson, he instructs them, as he did you in the *value* of freedom."[18]

More than a decade later, the Black Republic gained its freedom from European colonial rule as the slaves succeeded in overthrowing their masters.[19]

---

[17] Ibid.

[18] Ibid.

[19] Thomas Ott, *The Haitian Revolution, 1789-1804* (Knoxville: University of Tennessee Press, 1973); Laurent Dubois, *Avengers of the New World: The Story of the Haitian Revolution* (Cambridge: Belknap Press of Harvard University Press, 2004); Carolyn E. Fick, *The Making of Haiti: The Saint Domingue Revolution from Below* (Knoxville: University of Tennessee Press, 1990); C. L. R. James, *The Black Jacobins: Toussaint L'Ouverture and the San Domingo Revolution* (London: Allison

17

With the end of the revolution and the newly gained independence of Haiti occurring during the U.S. presidency of Thomas Jefferson, the author of the American Revolution's foundational document, race drove vision and action in two ways.

First, from a geopolitical and an ideological perspective, Jefferson established the precedent of not recognizing Haiti, despite it being the second republic in the New World.[20] The United States could not accept that purportedly inferior people could supposedly operate a superior form of government. As Toussaint L'Ouverture had astutely detected during Jefferson's administration, according to the account by the U.S. consul to Saint Domingue at the time, "He [L'Ouverture] immediately

---

and Busby, 1980); Malick Ghachem, *The Old Regime and the Haitian Revolution* (New York: Cambridge University Press, 2012); Philippe Girard, *The Slaves Who Defeated Napoleon* (Tuscaloosa: University of Alabama Press, 2011); Jeremy Popkin, *A Concise History of the Haitian Revolution* (Malden: Wiley-Blackwell, 2012); David Patrick Geggus, *Haitian Revolutionary Studies* (Bloomington: Indiana University Press, 2002).

[20] Arthur Scherr, *Thomas Jefferson's Haitian Policy: Myths and Realities* (New York: Lexington Books, 2011); Tim Matthewson, "Jefferson and Haiti," *The Journal of Southern History*, Vol. 61, No. 2 (May 1995), pp. 209.248.

returned my Commission without opening it, expressing his disappointment and disgust in strong terms, saying that his Colour was the cause of his being neglected, and not thought worthy of the Usual attentions."[21]

Second, besides the realm of national leadership, Jefferson thought in terms of a large slaveholder participating in the slaveholding society of Virginia. While the revolution on the island was still ongoing, he had written to James Madison expressing his fear of slave rebellion, "Against this, there is no remedy but timely measures on our part, to clear ourselves, by degrees, of the matter on which that lever can work." Jefferson had advocated for gradual emancipation, not necessarily out of a belief that people of African descent should also participate in republicanism, but rather out of self-preservation. He reinforced his fear of insurrection: "If something is not done, and soon done, we shall be the murderers of our children."[22]

---

[21] Tobias Lear to Secretary of State James Madison, 17 July 1801, accessed via http://thelouvertureproject.org/index.php?title=Tobias _Lear_letter_to_James_Madison .
[22] Thomas Jefferson to James Madison, 5 February 1799; in Paul L. Ford, ed., *The Writings of Thomas*

This slaveholder fear had significant impact, sparking reactions both private and public that affected social stances and political policies toward slavery.[23]

The Virginian planter John Taylor wrote a series of essays that were published in at least two editions shortly after Haiti gained independence.[24] He tried to shift the paradigm of slaveholding in the United States, where liberty was so cherished in rhetoric. The Revolutionary generation had continued slavery in an almost apologetic manner as a necessary evil. Jefferson had genuine moral

---

Jefferson, 10 vols., (New York: G.P. Putnam's Sons, 1892-90), 7.

[23] David Brion Davis, *The Slave Power Conspiracy and the Paranoid Style* (Baton Rouge: Louisiana State University Press, 1969); David Brion Davis, "Impact of the French and Haitian Revolutions," Seymour Drescher, "The Limits of Example," Robin Blackburn, "The Force of Example," and Simon P. Newman, "American Political Culture and the French and Haitian Revolutions: Nathaniel Cutting and the Jeffersonian Republicans," in David P. Geggus, ed., *The Impact of the Haitian Revolution in the Atlantic World* (Columbia: University of South Carolina Press, 2001), pp. 3-9, 10-14, 15-20, 72-89.

[24] John Taylor, *The Arator; Being a Series of Agricultural Essays, Practical and Political* (1814; New York: Liberty Classics, 1977).

struggles within himself over what he viewed as he and his cohort's failure. He hoped that the next generation would address the issue. To the contrary, Taylor argued for a new way of viewing slavery that framed it as a positive good. It was one of the earliest pro slavery arguments in the United States.[25]

This was, in essence, a way to shield against the type of reasoning advanced by Abraham Bishop of Connecticut. Assuming slavery to be the proper order of things (economic, social and political) Taylor contended that the act of enslaving people was not what had caused the rebellion in Haiti, but it rather the inciting rhetoric of the antislavery and abolitionist fringes that had caused such unrest.[26]

As Frederick Douglass would later recall about the antebellum period of the United States, "While slavery existed amongst us, her [Haiti's] example was a sharp thorn in our side and a source of alarm and terror. She came into the sisterhood of nations through blood. She

---

[25] John Taylor, *The Arator; Being a Series of Agricultural Essays, Practical and Political* (1814; New York: Liberty Classics, 1977), 52-5.
[26] Ibid.

was described at the time of her advent, as a very hell of horrors. Her very name was pronounced with a shudder. She was a startling and frightful surprise and a threat to all slave-holders throughout the world."[27] It was precisely this fear that would later manifest itself in the depiction of the so-called Black Republican conspiracies of the 1850s. These set the climate for secession from the Union once the Republican Party candidate Abraham Lincoln was elected as President. Taylor, in building the intellectual case supporting slavery, advocated that slavery be viewed as a permanent part of the nation, rather than a necessary evil eventually to be phased out.

Yet, white social and political leaders were not alone in defining Haiti by the colour of its residents' skin. This was especially once U.S. policy viewed Haiti through the prism of race, thus creating the box within which Haiti could be viewed. For example, in 1861, just before the outbreak of civil war in the United States, Frederick Douglass, the leading African American voice, pointed out

---

[27] Frederick Douglass, Lecture on Haiti, Chicago, 2 January 1893, accessed via http://www2.webster.edu/~corbetre/haiti/history/1844 -1915/douglass.htm .

"Both the press and the platform of the United States have long made Haiti the bugbear and scare-crow of the cause of freedom."[28] Consequently, someone like Douglass was conditioned to view Haiti through the lens of race. He looked proudly at Haiti as proof of the falsehoods perpetuated by white supremacy, which was precisely why it was ignored: "Though a city set on a hill, she has been hid."[29] In his framing of Haiti, Douglass was both profoundly American yet transcendent of U.S. nationalism. He bought into the U.S.-inspired concept of a republic as an example to the world (i.e. city on a hill), yet he also felt a sense of belonging to the African diaspora that extended far beyond the United States, for example, into Haiti.

U.S.-born, Fredrick Douglass, identified with others in the diaspora who had no connection to him whatsoever. This was not unlike the identity assigned to him and others, by white U.S. leaders, who refused to

---

[28] Frederick Douglass, *Douglass' Monthly*, May 1861; in Philip Foner and Yuval Taylor, eds., *Frederick Douglass: Selected Speeches and Writings* (New York: Lawrence Hill Books, 1999), 441.
[29] Ibid.

recognize Haiti by lumping black people on the island with black people in the United States as one race.

Simultaneous to such a broader association, Douglass, who had been subjected to slavery in a nation with high ideals, bought into that nation's proclaimed values and form of government such that it was used as a measuring stick to demonstrate that people with black skin could be just as civilized, advanced, and noble as those with white skin. Douglass further revealed this juxtaposition of his faith in the values of the United States, along with a sense of wider identification with the African diaspora, when he labeled Haiti as "the theatre of many stirring events and heroic achievements, the work of a people, bone of our bone, flesh of our flesh."[30]

These ideas of wider racial solidarity, American nationalism, and faith in republicanism intertwined together when he pointed to "the free, orderly and Independent Republic of Haiti" as "a refutation of the slanders and disparagements of our race."[31] Laced in that statement were rebuttals to black stereotypes as

---

[30] Douglass, *Douglass' Monthly*, May 1861, 440.
[31] Ibid.

disorderly and needing to depend on paternalistic white people for their well-being, a sense of African identity, and a strong assumption of U.S. values as well as a presumed accurate measuring tool of fellow humans as civilized.

For generations, African American voices simultaneously identified with a transcendent brotherhood of the black diaspora while still vindicating their envisioned people through Euro-American conceptions of civilization. In the young United States of the late eighteenth-century, a former slave who had organized one of the first and most prominent African American societies when he established the African Masonic Lodge in Boston, Prince Hall urged his black American "brethren" to maintain hope as they remembered "our African brethren" in the "French West-Indies" (i.e. Haiti) before its independence effort was even determined to be complete.[32] Invoking a common African place of origin with mythical status, he continued

---

[32] Prince Hall, "A Charge" (1797); in Richard Newman, Patrick Rael, and Philip Lapsansky, eds., *Pamphlets of Protest: An Anthology of Early African-American Protest Literature, 1790-1860* (New York: Routledge, 2001), 47.

with an optimistic narrative of unfolding improvement, "Thus doth Ethiopia begin to stretch forth her hand, from a sink of slavery to freedom and equality."[33] Similarly, a generation later, in one of the most important pamphlets published in antebellum United States, David Walker – born a free African American in North Carolina who later moved to Boston to work on the nation's first independent black newspaper based out of New York – referred to the white English, who had abolished slavery, as "our greatest and earthly friends and benefactors," while labeling "the Haitians" as "our brethren."[34] Another generation later, a pastor in Rhode Island who co-founded the Second Freewill Baptist Church, John W. Lewis, identified himself as "a colored man, and as a representative of the African race," even as he recognized a larger "human race" in the eyes of God while refuting the eugenics science of the American school.[35]

---

[33] Ibid.

[34] David Walker, "Appeal to the Colored Citizens of the World" (1830); in *Pamphlets of Protest*, 97.

[35] John W. Lewis, "Essay on the Character and Condition of the African Race" (1852); in John Lewis, *The Life, Labors, And Travels Of Elder Charles Bowles, Of The Free Will Baptist Denominations, By Eld. John W. Lewis. Together*

Lewis, like his contemporary Frederick Douglass, still relied on measuring civilization through Euro-American criteria. Lewis referred to "American or European cities" with populations of "refined improvement," when he argued that the conditions surrounding these civilizations were what allowed for the perceived advantages of these societies.[36] He explained, "So it is in the history of the human race, so that the superiority of one class over an inferior one, only the result of improved opportunity in becoming intelligent, in the progress of civilization."[37] Lewis and Douglass were not alone in buying into a European paradigm of civilization, nor was the critical link of applying this framework to Haiti as a vindication of black peoples lost on other leading African American voices.

With An Essay On The Character And Condition Of The African Race, By The Same. Also, An Essay On The Fugitive Law Of The U.S. Congress Of 1850, By Rev. Arthur Dearing (Watertown, CT: Ingalls & Stowell's Steam Press, 1852); in Pamphlets of Protest, 192.

[36] Lewis, "Essay on the Character and Condition of the African Race" (1852); in Pamphlets of Protest, 196.

[37] Ibid.

Born to free black parents in the U.S. District of Columbia, James Theodore Holly worked as a clerk for an abolitionist before even turning twenty years of age. He thus quickly grew to become a black nationalist and missionary who traveled and lived across the northern United States and Canada during his young adulthood. In a lecture published in 1857 by the Afric-American Printing Company, which had been established by the National Emigration Convention "for the purpose of publishing negro Literature,"[38]Holly measured Haiti by European standards of education, agriculture, economy, and trade. These criteria helped him argue, "Hence these evidences of educational and industrial development, expanding continually as years roll onward, we regard as the most irrefragable proof of true civilized progress on the part of the Haytian people."[39] Holly positioned the image of an

---

[38] J. Theodore Holly, "A Vindication of the Capacity of the Negro for Self-Government and Civilized Progress" (1857); in Rev. Jas. Theo. Holly, *A Vindication Of The Capacity Of The Negro Race For Self-Government, and Civilized Progress, As Demonstrated By The Historical Events Of The Haytian Revolution; And The Subsequent Acts Of That People Since Their National Independence* (New Haven: John P. Anthony, Agent. William H. Stanley, Printer, 1857); in *Pamphlets of Protest*, 280.

island in the sea within European impressions of civilization, "I have summoned the sable heroes and statesmen of that independent isle of the Caribbean Sea, and tried them by the high standard of modern civilization, fearlessly comparing them with the most illustrious men of the most enlightened nations on the earth."[40] Indeed, even the title of his address and publication, "A Vindication of the Capacity of the Negro for Self-Government and Civilized Progress"[41] revealed just how much Holly bought into European conceptions of what it meant to be civilized and attempted to judge the peoples of the world, particularly of African descent, by these notions. Thus, he concluded that he had proven "the Negro's equality with the white man carrying forward the great principles of self-government and

---

[39] Holly, "A Vindication of the Capacity of the Negro for Self-Government and Civilized Progress" (1857); in *Pamphlets of Protest*, 276.

[40] Holly, "A Vindication of the Capacity of the Negro for Self-Government and Civilized Progress" (1857); in *Pamphlets of Protest*, 278.

[41] Holly, "A Vindication of the Capacity of the Negro for Self-Government and Civilized Progress" (1857); in *Pamphlets of Protest*, 262-280.

civilized progress" as the "Negro race" had not fallen "one whit behind their contemporaries."[42]

Holly built much of his case toward charges of black inferiority that circulated particularly in the United States. In response to the paternalistic and condescending claim that black people could not govern themselves, he summarized over half a century of Haitian history since its independence "in demonstration of the Negro's ability to govern themselves."[43] Even during the revolution itself, prior to independence, black persons had shown a capacity to act with political savvy. Holly pointed out the "wise stratagems" of "colored deputies of St. Domingo" in Paris who had some success in the National Assembly of France, even "pressing a liberty-loving slaveholder into their service" in order to "thunder their measures through the National Assembly" with "a bold declaration."[44] He

[42] Holly, "A Vindication of the Capacity of the Negro for Self-Government and Civilized Progress" (1857); in *Pamphlets of Protest*, 278.

[43] Holly, "A Vindication of the Capacity of the Negro for Self-Government and Civilized Progress" (1857); in *Pamphlets of Protest*, 274.

[44] Holly, "A Vindication of the Capacity of the Negro for Self-Government and Civilized Progress" (1857); in *Pamphlets of Protest*, 268.

compared the able political achievement to a renowned institution of political maneuvering in the United States, "Who among the old fogies of Tammany Hall could have surpassed these tactics of those much abused men of color... And who, after this convincing proof to the contrary, shall dare to say that the negro race is not capable of self-government?"[45]

Holly also rebutted the common portrayal of black people as too easily drunk with power and thus prone to excess that would lead to a lack of stability. Again, he used the United States as the benchmark, when he highlighted that Haiti had eight executives in the preceding 53 years while the U.S. had ten in the prior 48 years.[46] He emphasized this point just as Frederick Douglass made sure to label Haiti as an "orderly"[47] republic. With the exception of the United States and Brazil, there was "no nation" in the Western Hemisphere, Holly contended, "that can pretend to compare with Hayti, in respect to general stability of government."[48] Of

[45] Ibid.

[46] Holly, "A Vindication of the Capacity of the Negro for Self-Government and Civilized Progress" (1857); in *Pamphlets of Protest*, 276.

[47] Douglass, *Douglass' Monthly*, May 1861, 440.

course, his emphasis on proving this stability as "another evidence of civilized progress"[49] only played into the gage imposed by Euro-Americans, just as when Holly indicated, "The desire for Republican institutions has its rise in the Cosmopolitan ideas and example of France, at the time of the Haytian Revolution." Like Douglass, Holly esteemed republicanism as a political philosophy.

Holly applied the Euro-American concept of republicanism to validate Haiti by matching it up to the ultimate of cherished republican movements – the American Revolution. "The Haytian Revolution is also the grandest political event of this or any other age," Holly declared, "In weighty causes, and wondrous and momentous features, it surpasses the American revolution, in an incomparable degree."[50] The revolution in the United States "was only the revolt of a people

---

[48] Holly, "A Vindication of the Capacity of the Negro for Self-Government and Civilized Progress" (1857); in *Pamphlets of Protest*, 277.

[49] Holly, "A Vindication of the Capacity of the Negro for Self-Government and Civilized Progress" (1857); in *Pamphlets of Protest*, 276.

[50] Holly, "A Vindication of the Capacity of the Negro for Self-Government and Civilized Progress" (1857); in *Pamphlets of Protest*, 264.

already comparatively free, independent, and highly enlightened. But the Haytian revolution was a revolt of an uneducated and menial class of slaves, against their tyrannical oppressors."[51] "These oppressors, against whom the negro insurgents of Hayti had to contend, were not only the government of a far distant mother country, as in the case of the American revolution," Holly continued, "but unlike and more fearful than this revolt, the colonial government of Hayti was also thrown in the balance against the negro revolters. The American revolters had their colonial government in their own hands, as well as their individual liberty at the commencement of the revolution. The black insurgents of Hayti had yet to grasp both their personal liberty and the control of their colonial government, by the might of their own right hands, when their heroic struggle began."[52] In short, Holly reckoned, "The obstacles to surmount, and the difficulties to contend against, in the American revolution, when compared to those of the Haytian, were, (to use a homely but classic phrase,) but a 'tempest in a

---

[51] Ibid.
[52] Ibid.

teapot,' compared to the dark and lurid thunder storm of the dissolving heavens."[53]

Despite such a challenging atmosphere, black leaders maintained their poise, as Holly further refuted the charge against the ability of black people to maintain mature composure. As he explained, "The exceptional part which the blacks played in the moving drama that was then being enacted in St. Domingo, by their stern self-possession amid the furious excitement of the whites, is one of the strongest proofs that can be adduced to substantiate the capabilities of the negro race for self-government."[54] The figurative black man, Holly reiterated, "remained heedless of the effervescence of liberty that bubbled over in the bosom of the white man; and continued at his sullen labors, biding his time for deliverance… When we look upon this characteristic of cool, self-possession, we cannot but regard it as almost a miracle under the circumstances. We cannot see what magic power could keep such a warm blooded race of

---

[53] Ibid.
[54] Holly, "A Vindication of the Capacity of the Negro for Self-Government and Civilized Progress" (1857); in *Pamphlets of Protest*, 265-266.

men in such an ice bound spell of cold indifference, when every other class of men in that colony was flush with excitement of *liberty*."[55] These self-possessed black men were not "indifferent" because they were "too ignorant to appreciate the blessings of liberty," nor were they "quiet" because they were "too cowardly to strike their disenthrallment" – instead, their "judicious reserve" revealed "one of the strongest traits of self-government."[56] As a result of such powerful evidence, Holly proclaimed, "Nothing shall rob of the immaculate glory of exhibiting a stern self-possession, in that feverish hour of excitement, when every body around them were crying out Liberty. And in this judicious self-control at this critical juncture, when their destiny hung on the decision of the hour, we have a brilliant illustration of the capacity of the race for self-government."[57] Black people had demonstrated a capability for restrained self-discipline in the midst of an environment both impassioned and disorderly.

---

[55] Holly, "A Vindication of the Capacity of the Negro for Self-Government and Civilized Progress" (1857); in *Pamphlets of Protest*, 266.
[56] Ibid.
[57] Ibid.

Black leaders in the Haitian revolt were a critical element to Holly's rebuttal of the representations of the specter of "negro rule" in the United States. Toussaint L'Ouverture had displayed a "genius… to meet an emergency that no other man in the world was so peculiarly prepared to fulfill; and thereby he has added another inextinguishable proof of the capacity of the negro for self-government."[58] Under his governorship, Haiti had reached "the highest degree of prosperity it ever attained,"[59] despite centuries of European colonial governance. The "godlike Toussaint" was an excellent leader but not a black man with extraordinary capacity, as Holly drew attention to black Haitians "producing other leaders to fill up the gap now left open" and hence "the race again proved itself equal to the emergency" at hand.[60]

---

[58] Holly, "A Vindication of the Capacity of the Negro for Self-Government and Civilized Progress" (1857); in *Pamphlets of Protest*, 271-272.

[59] Holly, "A Vindication of the Capacity of the Negro for Self-Government and Civilized Progress" (1857); in *Pamphlets of Protest*, 272.

[60] Holly, "A Vindication of the Capacity of the Negro for Self-Government and Civilized Progress" (1857); in *Pamphlets of Protest*, 274.

Still, even outside of redefining Haiti in particular, African American leaders could not seem to escape the paradigm of Euro-American civilization. An early voice for Pan Africanism, Alexander Crummell, educated at Cambridge University, felt African Americans could introduce Christianity and civilization in West Africa to bring the continent into the modern world by championing the English language he found so rich in its concepts of liberty and human rights. The English language, with "ITS HIGH MORAL AND SPIRITUAL CHARACTER," Crummell maintained, could cultivate "that sensitive honor, those habits of honest, that purity of manners and morals, those domestic virtues, and that evangelical piety, which are peculiarly attributes of Anglo-Saxon society, States and homes."[61] While men like J. Theodore Holly and Frederick Douglass may not have emphasized "the great and ennobling ENGLISH LANGUAGE"[62] as Crummell did, they did buy into

---

[61] Alexander Crummell, "The English Language in Liberia" (1861); in Rev. Alexander Crummell, B.A., *The English Language in Liberia*, The Annual Address Before the Citizens of Maryland County, Cape Palmas, Liberia – July 26, 1860 (New York: Bunce & Co., 1861); in *Pamphlets of Protest*, 303.
[62] Ibid.

measuring black peoples by a standard invented by white peoples. When Crummell made sure to refer to Liberia as "the Republic,"[63] he did not sound unlike the similar labeling of Haiti by Douglass and Holly as they prized republicanism. Like these two men, Crummell touted "an organized negro community, republican in form and name;" and like John W. Lewis, too, he cherished "a people possessed of Christian institutions and civilized habits."[64] Indeed, Douglass, Holly, and Lewis did not speak specifically of "rude natives" in Africa,[65] but neither did they mention these peoples as part of their rebuttals to white depictions of black peoples, choosing instead to highlight black people who fit the characteristics of civilization, progress, and refinement set by white Europeans and Americans. Rather than refute the imposed paradigm altogether, they boasted of what Crummell called "the Anglican aspect of our habits and manners."[66] Unlike the "West African Pagans,"[67] when

---

[63] Crummell, "The English Language in Liberia" (1861); in *Pamphlets of Protest*, 286.
[64] Crummell, "The English Language in Liberia" (1861); in *Pamphlets of Protest*, 285.
[65] Ibid.
[66] Ibid.
[67] Ibid.

looking at peoples of African descent who had sufficiently Europeanized, "There could be no mistaking the history of this people."[68]

Therein lies the crux of the juxtaposition: claiming a history. The modern political scientist James C. Scott writes from an applicable framework when he describes "Zomia," which is "the largest remaining region of the world whose peoples have not yet been fully incorporated into nation-states."[69] He presents a recovery history that endeavors to assign agency and voice to those who have long been assumed (and sometimes asserted) by neighbors and scholars to have little or no history. In doing so, Scott strives to remove his historical subjects from the paradigm of primitive barbarism, a key component of which entails reducing a people with the indictment of lacking history; "Stateless peoples are typically stigmatized by neighboring cultures as 'peoples without history,' as lacking the fundamental characteristic of civilization, namely historicity."[70] Therefore, African

---

[68] Crummell, "The English Language in Liberia" (1861); in *Pamphlets of Protest*, 285-286.
[69] James C. Scott, *The Art of Not Being Governed: An Anarchist History of Upland Southeast Asia* (New Haven: Yale University Press, 2009), ix.

American leaders who represented a people barbarized through slavery by the nineteenth-century attempted to identify a history so they too could have an origin, past, and development as hallmarks of civilization – a human history rather than a dark savagery charged to their peoples. However, in doing so, rather than re-conceptualizing a history as Scott does to the peoples of Zomia, these African American leaders argued on the terms of those who had robbed African peoples of their history in the first place. They outlined a history that impressed European paradigms, upheld the beliefs of progress and civilization dictated by those in power, and overlooked the possibility that history could have been a tool for the state.   Thus these peoples may have used a lack of what Westerners deemed as history as a form of resistance to incorporation into the rising early modern hegemonies based in Europe. As Scott points out, "Virtually everything about these people's livelihoods, social organization, ideologies, and (more controversially) even their largely oral cultures, can be read as strategic positions designed to keep the state at arm's length."[71]

---

[70] Scott, *The Art of Not Being Governed*, 237.
[71] Scott, *The Art of Not Being Governed*, x.

Accordingly, "Relatively powerless hill peoples… may well find it to their advantage to avoid written traditions and fixed texts, or even to abandon them altogether, in order to maximize their room for cultural maneuver. The shorter their genealogies and histories the less they have to explain and the more they can invent on the spot."[72] These African American producers of black histories on the terms of white sensibilities may have failed to notice who Scott looks back upon and recognizes: "Not so very long ago, however, such self-governing people were the great majority of humankind,"[73] and they decided "how much history" (decipherable by European models) to have through "an active choice" rather than a unplanned product of a "low stage of evolution."[74]

Consequently, black American leaders in the United States attempted to outline and identify with a history of black people that met the standards of Euro-American civilization. For example, J. Theodore Holly, who delivered a lecture demonstrating "the capacity of the Negro for self-government and civilized progress," turned

[72] Scott, *The Art of Not Being Governed*, 235.
[73] Scott, *The Art of Not Being Governed*, ix.
[74] Scott, *The Art of Not Being Governed*, 237.

41

to history to prove his point: "The task that I propose to myself in the present lecture, is an earnest attempt to defend the inherent capabilities of the negro race, for self-government and civilized progress. For this purpose, I will examine the events of Haytian History, from the commencement of the revolution to the present period."[75] Beyond representing noble achievements of the African diaspora, Haiti provided a history with which black peoples could feel on par with white narratives of civilization. It was not only a place that had a history, which in itself was something to cherish, according to the paradigm of civilization imagined by Europeans, but Haiti's history was worthy of distinction, as Holly explained it. He declared, "This revolution is one of the noblest, grandest, and most justifiable outbursts against tyrannical oppression that is recorded on the pages of the world's history."[76] As he substantiated, "Never before, in all the annals of the world's history, did a nation of abject

---

[75] Holly, "A Vindication of the Capacity of the Negro for Self-Government and Civilized Progress" (1857); in *Pamphlets of Protest*, 263

[76] Holly, "A Vindication of the Capacity of the Negro for Self-Government and Civilized Progress" (1857); in *Pamphlets of Protest*, 264.

and chattel slavery arise in the terrific might of their resuscitated manhood, and regenerate, redeem, and disenthrall themselves; by taking their station at one gigantic bound, as an independent nation, among the sovereignties of the world."[77] Accordingly, Holly went on to provide a detailed history from the preliminary events of the revolution through to its aftermath, along the way analyzing from different angles in order to show the many layers of this history worthy of praise.[78]

Critical to making this history useable for African Americans in the United States was an identification with a larger black race – a categorization created by white supremacist ideology, yet seized upon by black American leaders when using these classifications to their advantage. Without feeling as part of a larger black diaspora, Holly would not have been able to contend as he did, "Our brethren of Hayti, who stand in the vanguard of the race, have already made a name, and a fame for us, that is as imperishable as the world's history."[79] This

[77] Ibid.

[78] Holly, "A Vindication of the Capacity of the Negro for Self-Government and Civilized Progress" (1857); in *Pamphlets of Protest*, 264-279.

[79] Holly, "A Vindication of the Capacity of the Negro

43

sense of brotherhood allowed him to apply the noble history to who he recognized as his people when assigning them a history that measured up with that of Europeans. Hence, upon concluding his "historical investigations," Holly affirmed that he had "now fulfilled my design in vindicating the capacity of the negro race for self-government and civilized progress against the unjust aspersions of our unprincipled oppressors, by boldly examining the facts of Haytian history, and deducing legitimate conclusions therefrom."[80] The shedding of a common blood had consecrated this historic achievement, "That freedom and independence are written in the world's history in the ineffaceable characters of blood; and it's crimson letters will ever testify to the determination and of the ability of the negro to be free, throughout the everlasting succession of ages."[81] Holly had crafted a black history of the world and for the world.

---

for Self-Government and Civilized Progress" (1857); in *Pamphlets of Protest*, 278.
[80] Ibid.
[81] Holly, "A Vindication of the Capacity of the Negro for Self-Government and Civilized Progress" (1857); in *Pamphlets of Protest*, 274.

This history also served as an instructive lesson to those who perpetuated the dehumanization of enslaved black people. "No historian has yet done them justice,"[82] avowed William Wells Brown, a former slave and conductor on the Underground Railroad, as he presented a lecture in 1854 that emphasized the roles of color and caste in a thorough account of the Haitian Revolution.[83] He warned, "Let the slave-holders in our Southern States tremble when they shall call to mind these events," after he had described the widespread violence during the fight for freedom in Haiti.[84]

Like Abraham Bishop before him, and like his contemporary J. Theodore Holly, Brown invoked the principles of the U.S. American Revolution, "The

---

[82] William Wells Brown, "The History of the Haitian Revolution" (1855); in William Wells Brown, *St. Domingo: Its Revolutions and its Patriots. A Lecture, Delivered Before the Metropolitical Athenaeum, London, May 16, and at St. Thomas' Church, Philadelphia, December 20, 1854* (Boston: Bela March, 1855); in *Pamphlets of Protest*, 252.
[83] Brown, "The History of the Haitian Revolution" (1855); in *Pamphlets of Protest*, 241-253.
[84] Brown, "The History of the Haitian Revolution" (1855); in *Pamphlets of Protest*, 249.

revolution that was commenced in 1776 would then be finished, and the glorious sentiments of the Declaration of Independence, 'That all men are created equal, and endowed by their Creator with certain inalienable rights, among which are life, liberty, and the pursuit of happiness,' would be realized."[85] Like Frederick Douglass and others, Brown deeply bought into the proclaimed ideals of the very nation that oppressed him. However, Brown went further, and like Bishop's scathing articles published soon after the U.S. revolutionary period amidst the unfolding revolution in Haiti, he justified bloodshed within the context of the violent revolt by the United States against the British empire. As Brown contended, "If the blacks [in Haiti] were guilty of shedding blood profusely, they only followed the example set them by the more refined and educated whites."[86] And in speaking of enslaved black people in the U.S. South, Brown surmised, "That their souls are thirsting for liberty, all will admit."[87] The spirit of the revolution that created the

---

[85] Brown, "The History of the Haitian Revolution" (1855); in *Pamphlets of Protest*, 253.
[86] Brown, "The History of the Haitian Revolution" (1855); in *Pamphlets of Protest*, 252.
[87] Ibid.

46

United States had already permeated among African Americans, as he deduced, "What the Helots were to Sparta at the time of the earthquake, the blacks were to St. Domingo at the time of the French revolution. And the American slaves are only waiting for the opportunity of wiping out their wrongs in the blood of their oppressors."[88] Therefore, Brown argued, as he looked both backward and forward, "The spirit that caused the blacks to take up arms, and to shed their blood in the American revolutionary war, is still amongst the slaves of the south; and, if we are not mistaken, the day is not far distant when the revolution of St. Domingo will be reenacted in South Carolina and Louisiana."[89] That was precisely what had scared Thomas Jefferson, who acknowledged the contradiction between the words he had penned and the actions of that country. In fact, Brown cited Jefferson: "In contemplating the fact that the slave would rise and vindicate his right to freedom by physical force, Jefferson said:– 'Indeed, I tremble for my country when I reflect that God is just, that his justice cannot sleep forever; that, considering numbers, nature, and natural means only, a

---

[88] Ibid.
[89] Ibid.

revolution of the wheel of fortune, and exchange of situation, is among possible events; that it may become probable by supernatural interference! The Almighty has no attribute which can take side with us in such a contest.'... And should such a contest take place, the God of Justice will be on the side of the oppressed blacks."[90] Haiti had already proven so.

As one of the most outspoken black leaders of the antebellum era, Henry Highland Garnet also advocated for a more direct resistance. As the former slave addressed, "Brethren, it is as wrong for your lordly oppressors to keep you in slavery, as it was for the man thief to steal our ancestor from the coast of Africa... Brethren, the time has come when you must act for yourselves."[91] After remembering slave rebellions in the United States, Garnet called, "Noble men! Those who' have fallen in freedom's conflict, their memories will be

---

[90] Brown, "The History of the Haitian Revolution" (1855); in *Pamphlets of Protest*, 253. Brown was quoting Jefferson from *Notes on the State of Virginia*, first published in 1781.

[91] Henry Highland Garnet, "Address to the Slaves of the United States" (1848); in *Pamphlets of Protest*, 162.

cherished by the true-hearted and the God-fearing in all future generations; those who are living, their names are surrounded by a halo of glory. Brethren, arise, arise! Strike for your lives and liberties... *Rather die freemen than live to be slaves*... In the name of God, we ask, are you men?"[92] When this address was considered at a black national convention in Buffalo in 1843, it received significant opposition, primarily by Frederick Douglass, who according to the minutes of the meeting, pointed out, "that there was too much physical force."[93] The disagreements among African American leaders extended beyond the question of aggression.

Douglass venerated Haiti, but he did not support colonization efforts to the Black Republic. His planned trip in 1861 was not only to "do justice to Haiti, to paint her as she is," but also due to the "state of things at present existing in this country."[94] He pointed out that free black people in the United States, had seemingly diminishing opportunity in the North, and in the South they were told

---

[92] Garnet, "Address to the Slaves of the United States" (1848); in *Pamphlets of Protest*, 164.
[93] "Debate over Garnet's 'Address to the Slaves of the United States'" (1848); in *Pamphlets of Protest*, 158.
[94] Douglass, *Douglass' Monthly*, May 1861, 441.

to choose between slavery or expulsion. Consequently, he reasoned, they were "now, as never before, looking out into the world for a place of retreat, an asylum from the apprehended storm which is about to beat pitilessly upon them."[95] Douglass, in this particular instance, did not bother "attempting to dispel this apprehension by appeals to facts, which have failed to satisfy, and to general principles of development of progress, which most of our people have deemed too abstract and transcendental for practical life."[96] Instead, for those "already resolved to look for homes beyond the boundaries of the United States," he would visit Haiti in order to gather more information, "without at all discrediting the statements of others," many of whom he believed to be "individuals of the highest character and respectability."[97] Yet, even in disapproving of black emigration from the United States, Douglass framed Haiti as the "modern land of Canaan, where so many of our people are journeying from the rigorous bondage and oppression of our modern Egypt."[98] Haiti represented a

[95] Ibid.
[96] Douglass, *Douglass' Monthly*, May 1861, 442.
[97] Ibid.
[98] Ibid.

sanctuary for black freedom from slavery, even by the man who opposed escaping to the iconic republic; and the United States was Egypt in that story, even by the man who so fervently believed in the ideals and values of that same oppressor nation.

Emigration was an issue hotly debated by African American leaders, and the Black Republic was an important part of that conversation. For example, as Henry Highland Garnet urged resistance by slaves against their masters, he also advocated leaving the United States.[99] Additionally, Alexander Crummell called for colonization in Liberia as a frontier of civilization in West Africa.[100] On the other hand, like Frederick Douglass, David Walker maintained, "This country is as much ours as it is the whites, whether they will admit it now or not."[101] Emigration, he worried, would get free black people "away from among those of our brethren whom they [slaveholders] unjustly hold in bondage, so that they may

---

[99] Garnet, "Address to the Slaves of the United States" (1848); in *Pamphlets of Protest*, 156.
[100] Crummell, "The English Language in Liberia" (1861), in *Pamphlets of Protest*, 282.
[101] Walker, "Appeal to the Colored Citizens of the World" (1830); in *Pamphlets of Protest*, 97.

be enabled to keep them the more secure in ignorance and wretchedness, to support them and their children, and consequently they would have the more obedient slaves."[102] However, J. Theodore Holly argued for the civilization of Haiti in order to persuade fellow black Americans to move to Haiti. He was a missionary and Protestant Episcopal Bishop of Haiti who resided on the island for decades. Cherishing "with due deference to the republican ideas which surround me," Holly pointed out the shortcomings of republican governance in the United States that had allowed for policies like the fugitive slave law.[103] "But such a determined spirit of liberty does not exist here" in the United States, Holly contended, "and honest men must submit therefore with lamb-like patience to this republican despotism of irresponsible political partisans who violate every just principal of law, because these unrighteous decrees are perpetrated in the name of the sovereign people."[104] Therefore, compared

---

[102] Walker, "Appeal to the Colored Citizens of the World" (1830); in *Pamphlets of Protest*, 92.
[103] Holly, "A Vindication of the Capacity of the Negro for Self-Government and Civilized Progress" (1857); in *Pamphlets of Protest*, 277.
[104] Holly, "A Vindication of the Capacity of the Negro for Self-Government and Civilized Progress"

to a corrupted republic, "there is far more security for personal liberty and the general welfare of the governed, among the monarchical negroes of Hayti where the rulers are held individually responsible for their public acts, than exists in this bastard democracy."[105] Still, Holly again revealed, as he did throughout his address, how strongly he believed in white visions of civilization. "We have work now to do here in the Western World," he encouraged, so black Americans must "go and identify our destiny with our heroic brethren in that independent isle of the Caribbean Sea, carrying with us such of the arts, sciences and genius of modern civilization, as we may gain from this hardy and enterprising Anglo-American race, in order to add to Haytian advancement."[106] For Holly, advocating emigration to Haiti was not only a way to leave behind the oppression of the United States, but it was also a Pan-African calling to help others in the black diaspora – Haiti signified both a refuge and a purpose.

(1857); in *Pamphlets of Protest*, 278.
[105] Ibid.
[106] Holly, "A Vindication of the Capacity of the Negro for Self-Government and Civilized Progress" (1857); in *Pamphlets of Protest*, 279.

Black emigration was a concept that was also favored by certain groups of white people, each for different reasons. Abraham Lincoln had long favored colonizing African Americans outside of the United States, even before he took office as the President of the United States.[107] Thus, not surprisingly, in the spring of 1862, he successfully pushed for a bill that allowed for both the compensation of slaveholders in the District of Columbia as well as the colonization of newly freed former enslaved people. Lincoln found the issue significant enough that he promoted it in his annual message to Congress during this period.[108] Congress appropriated funding to colonize consenting freedmen in Haiti and Liberia[109] – something

---

[107] Charles H. Wesley, "Lincoln's Plan for Colonizing the Emancipated Negroes," *The Journal of Negro History*, Vol. 4, No. 1 (Jan. 1919), pp. 7-21; Paul J. Scheips, "Lincoln and the Chiriqui Colonization Project," *The Journal of Negro History*, Vol. 37, No. 1 (Oct. 1952), pp. 418-453; Michael Vorenberg, "Abraham Lincoln and the Politics of Black Colonization," *Journal of the Abraham Lincoln Association*, Vol. 14, No. 2 (Summer 1993), pp. 22-45.

[108] Abraham Lincoln, Annual Message to Congress, December 1862; in Andrew Delbanco, ed., *The Portable Abraham Lincoln* (New York: Penguin Books, 2009).

Holly did not forget when Lincoln issued the Emancipation Proclamation and mentioned the option of colonization within the brief document. After the issuance of the preliminary Emancipation Proclamation, just weeks before the finalized Emancipation Proclamation would take effect, and just months before the United States finally recognized Haiti as a nation, a New York editor and politician wrote President Lincoln about his "friend" Bernard Kock, Governor of Vache Island, who "has before the Government a proposition for colonizing the Island, and that it is very desirable that the matter should be pressed forward as quickly as possible."[110] This provided a glimpse into how U.S. leaders viewed Haiti. Still defined by race, and therefore the place deemed appropriate to send black Americans, who were still not accepted as part of the United States, despite generations of presence. After failed attempts of colonization at a significant level, amidst a civil war sparked by the central issue of slavery,

---

[109] 37th Congress, 2nd Session.
[110] William E. Robinson to Abraham Lincoln, 13 December 1862, Abraham Lincoln Papers, Library of Congress, accessed via http://memory.loc.gov/ammem/alhtml/malcap.html .

the United States finally recognized Haiti – six decades after the creation of the Black Republic.

Still, U.S. relations with Haiti were not strong, nor was its cultural place in the minds of leading African Americans diminished after formal recognition. In his old age, Frederick Douglass still valued Haiti, as the passion by black Americans for this black iconic nation was never about geopolitics, but rather about its symbol for the black race. Nowhere in their words did African American leaders indicate that they had coalesced around Haiti due to non-recognition by the United States; they were driven by their fight against racism rather than a desire for appropriate foreign policy. Nevertheless, in an extended public speech about Haiti at the World's Fair in Chicago in 1893, Douglass touched on foreign policy: "A deeper reason for coolness between the two countries is this: Haiti is black, and we have not yet forgiven Haiti for being black (applause) or forgiven the Almighty for making her black. (Applause.)"[111] Douglass went on to single out the

---

[111] Douglass, Lecture on Haiti, Chicago, 2 January 1893, accessed via
http://www2.webster.edu/~corbetre/haiti/history/1844 -1915/douglass.htm .

particularly U.S. brand of racism, "In this enlightened act of repentance and forgiveness, our boasted civilization is far behind all other nations. (Applause.) In every other country on the globe a citizen of Haiti is sure of civil treatment (Applause.)"[112] He went on to encourage a stronger relationship between the United States and Haiti, pointing to Haiti's rich resources, people, and culture.

Even after more than three decades of U.S. recognition of Haiti, Douglass still felt the need to use Haiti to refute the white American racist images of black people. He acknowledged the racially driven questions that surrounded the perceptions of the Black Republic in that they were discussed in a context of both "Haiti and the possibilities of the negro race generally."[113] Images of black savages infused the projections of some, as Douglass recounted, "They tell us that Haiti is already doomed – that she is on the down-grade to barbarism... The argument stated against Haiti, is, that since her freedom, she has become lazy; that she is given to gross idolatry, and that these evils are on the increase... that

[112] Ibid.
[113] Ibid.

children are fatted for slaughter and offered as sacrifices to their voodoo deities; that large boys and girls run naked through the streets."[114] He rebutted each of these particular charges, sometimes appealing to logical observation and other times pointing out double standards. For example, Douglass remarked that Haiti could not be lazy, "No one can see the ships afloat in the splendid harbors of Haiti, and see the large imports and exports of the country, without seeing also that somebody there has been to work."[115] He also called attention to the fact that "superstition and idolatry in one form or another" was pervasive throughout the world, including white Europe. In mighty England, "Queen Victoria gets water from the Jordan to christen her children, as if the water of that river were any better than the water of any other river."[116] Or, in the United States, "We build houses and call them God's houses, and go into them to meet God, as if the Almighty dwelt in temples made with men's hands."[117] Therefore, it seemed clear to Douglass that "if men are denied a future civilization

---

[114] Ibid.
[115] Ibid.
[116] Ibid.
[117] Ibid.

because of superstition, there are other than the people of Haiti who must be so denied."[118]

However, Douglass still could not escape a Euro-American framework of civilization, as he admitted that Haiti was "an infant," that was still progressing.[119] White Americans in the United States, apparently having forgotten about their own civil war just a generation earlier, as well as two assassinated executives in the republic's short lifespan, still viewed Haiti's turbulence as an inability of black people to govern. Douglass urged them to "look into the history of the progress of other nations. Some of the most enlightened and highly civilized states of the world of today, were, a few centuries ago, as deeply depraved in morals, manners and customs, as Haiti is alleged to be now."[120] For evidence, he looked to Prussia, France, England, Italy, and Spain. Within that context, Douglass plead, "Give her time! Give her time! ... With a people beginning a national life as Haiti did, with such crude material within, and such antagonistic forces operating upon her from without, the marvel is, not that

[118] Ibid.
[119] Ibid.
[120] Ibid.

she is far in the rear of civilization, but that she has survived in any sense as a civilized nation."[121] Douglass predicted that Haiti would "yet be tall and strong... and, like the star of the north, will shine on and shine on forever. (Prolonged applause.)"[122] The Black Republic has a history of persisting and progressing, and he insisted that it would follow the same noble course as the nations he mentioned.

In such a contention for a particular narrative of civilization, Douglass appealed heavily to the history of Haiti as a point of vindication, as had so many African American leaders for generations. In this case, he did not narrate a history of Haiti in order to give it a history – an element so critical to the European notion of civilization – but rather he redeemed its history within a broader global context that included some of the key benchmarks of Western civilization. Douglass proclaimed, "In Greek or Roman history nobler daring cannot be found," when referring to the slave uprising that sparked the Haitian Revolution.[123] Earlier in Douglass' lifetime, William Well

---

[121] Ibid.
[122] Ibid.
[123] Ibid.

Brown had made a similar argument that "no revolution ever turned up greater heroes than that of St. Domingo."[124] Brown had gone on to compare Toussaint L'Ouverture to the towering European legend, Napoleon Bonaparte: "Toussaint fought for liberty; Napoleon fought for himself. Toussaint gained fame by leading an oppressed and injured race to the successful vindication of their rights; Napoleon made himself a name and acquired a scepter by supplanting liberty and destroying nationalities, in order to substitute his own illegitimate despotism."[125] Therefore, as Douglass maintained decades later, there was "reason to respect Haiti for her services to the cause of liberty and human equality throughout the world."[126] The Black Republic has played a critical role in the trajectory of the world's history:

> *"Until she spoke no Christian nation had abolished negro slavery. Until she spoke no christian nation*

---

[124] Brown, "The History of the Haitian Revolution" (1855); in *Pamphlets of Protest*, 252.

[125] Brown, "The History of the Haitian Revolution" (1855); in *Pamphlets of Protest*, 252-253.

[126] Douglass, Lecture on Haiti, Chicago, 2 January 1893, accessed via http://www2.webster.edu/~corbetre/haiti/history/1844-1915/douglass.htm .

had given to the world an organized effort to abolish slavery. Until she spoke the slave ship, followed by hungry sharks, greedy to devour the dead and dying slaves flung overboard to feed them, plouged in peace the South Atlantic painting the sea with the Negro's blood. Until she spoke, the slave trade was sanctioned by all the Christian nations of the world, and our land of liberty and light included. Men made fortunes by this infernal traffic, and were esteemed as good Christians, and the standing types and representations of the Saviour of the World. Until Haiti spoke, the church was silent, and the pulpit was dumb."[127]

In this respect, Douglass advocated, Haiti must be remembered in history, not only in the past, but moving forward. Like the ancient nations, Haiti "has had her mission in the world, and a mission which the world had much need to learn. She has taught the world the danger of slavery and the value of liberty."[128] Similarly, Brown had stated, "While Toussaint's memory will be revered by

---

[127] Ibid.
[128] Ibid.

all lovers of freedom, Napoleon's will be detested."[129] Douglass proclaimed, "She has grandly served the cause of universal human liberty... Their swords were not drawn and could not be drawn simply for themselves alone. They were linked and interlinked with their race, and striking for their freedom, they struck for the freedom of every black man in the world. (Prolonged applause.)"[130]

Clearly, African American leaders could not interpret the history of the Black Republic without focusing on the race of its people – and neither could white American leaders. Neither white nor black Americans had a united voice, but all viewed and interpreted Haiti through the lens of race. Some white leaders feared Haiti and denounced or ignored it. Others related it to the revolt in the name of liberty carried out against England that created the United States. Some black leaders looked to Haiti with hope for black peoples across the world, while others used that hope as reason

---

[129] Brown, "The History of the Haitian Revolution" (1855); in *Pamphlets of Protest*, 253.

[130] Douglass, Lecture on Haiti, Chicago, 2 January 1893, accessed via http://www2.webster.edu/~corbetre/haiti/history/1844-1915/douglass.htm .

to consider it a place of refuge from the oppression they suffered in their homeland. A a few even invoked it as a dangerous reminder to white leaders of what could become of the United States if the enslavement of African Americans endured. Yet, even in resistance, these African American leaders revealed how profoundly U.S. American they were in their republican values, and just how much they assumed Euro-American concepts of civilization as the premise for measuring proper development. Geopolitics mattered little; instead of a crusade for U.S. recognition of Haiti, what emerged and persisted was an effort to create an identity that black people could appreciate – perhaps venerate. Race was inseparable from imagining, viewing, and understanding the Black Republic, because, as Frederick Douglass noted, "The people of Haiti, by reason of ancestral identity, are more interesting to the colored people of the United States than to all others, for the Negro, like the Jew, can never part with his identity and race."[131]

---

[131] Ibid.

"The Knights of Labor – What They Aim At?"

A Labor Organization at its Peak

The Noble Order of the Knights of Labor reached its peak in 1886 with over six-hundred-thousand members, five-hundred-thousand of whom had just joined that year – the labor organization was growing at an incredible pace.[132] As the first interracial union, the Knights of Labor fought on behalf of labor, black or white. Thus, when the Knights convened for the General Assembly (the national convention) of 1886 in Richmond, Virginia, many black members attended. Some of the actions around Richmond by these delegates, but more particularly their actions during the convention itself, disturbed the South's social norms.

Most importantly, the introduction of General Master Workman Terence V. Powderly by Frank J. Ferrell of District Assembly 49 – the introduction of a white man by a black man – brought forth questions regarding the social statement the Knights were trying to make. Were the Knights of Labor trying to challenge the rules of "social equality" in the South? Were the Knights of Labor

---

[132] Alexander Saxton, *The Rise and Fall of the White Republic: Class Politics and Mass Culture in Nineteenth-Century America* (New York, 1990), 304.

promoting what white Southerners perceived to be "social equality" between the races?[133]

Even before the convention, Powderly had never advocated for anything beyond solidarity for the labor movement – across color lines indeed, but also a host of other potential societal lines, such as religion, political affiliation, or nationality. As he wrote in a letter months before the convention, "I want it understood that this order recognizes no color or creed, no nationality or religion, no politics or party."[134] Race, was like many other potentially dividing factors, according to Powderly: it must not hinder the advancement of labor. He had no particular interest in race beyond that incentive.

To historians focusing on race, the Order, especially under Powderly's leadership, may seem keen to advancing black rights to some extent. Yet, to view the

---

[133] The significance of the term "social equality" at the time will be explained in this essay. Additionally, its vague meaning will be elaborated throughout the story as it was often used by the historical characters themselves.

[134] Letter, 13 April 1886, Powderly Papers, in Philip Foner and Ronald Lewis, eds., *The Black Worker During the Era of the Knights of Labor*, volume III of the series *The Black Worker: A Documentary History from Colonial Times to the Present* (Philadelphia, 1978) 253.

Knights only as an interracial union is wrong-headed because it uses hindsight with anachronistic concerns in mind. In 1886, the organization advocated rights on behalf of labor regardless of many social distinctions – and race was only one example of such a line. Even the organization's previous head, Uriah Stephens, had declared, "I can see ahead of me an organization that will include men and women of every craft, creed, and color."[135] Thus, to call the organization's stance a "doctrine of interracial solidarity," as C. Vann Woodward did, is to be focused too much on that particular issue.[136] The Knights of Labor made an effort not only to be interracial, but also to be all-inclusive of labor – unlike, for example, the incipient American Federation of Labor. The reason race was highlighted from the Knights multi-faceted inclusive platform was not because the organization or its leadership cared to intentionally challenge racial norms. Rather, when the Order held its convention in Richmond in its effort to continue recruiting Southern members, the location of that event made the particular social line of

---

[135] Uriah Stephens, quoted, Robert E. Weir, *Beyond Labor's Veil: The Culture of the Knights of Labor* (University Park, Pennsylvania), 46.
[136] C. Vann Woodward, *Origins of the New South, 1877-1913* (Louisiana State University Press, 1951), 229.

race stick out and become an issue. It was not the Knights who made race a particular issue; it was, instead, the historical contingency of the location of the event that made it so.[137]

Still, on the specific issue of race, when it came up, Powderly made himself clear. Four years before the Richmond convention, Powderly wrote in a letter, "Our organization makes no difference with the outside color of the man, if he is white on the inside it is all we ask." Such a declaration made evident Powderly's combination of white supremacy and labor solidarity. As he would contend in a letter a year later, "Brothers remember that when capital strikes a blow at us it does not strike at the white working man, or the black working man, but it strikes at *Labor*." [138] The real issue was clearly labor.

---

[137] For example, the Knights of Labor also had religious turmoil, as that was one of the social lines it sought to cross in its goal for unification of labor. See: Robert E. Weir, *Knights Unhorsed: Internal Conflict in a Gilded Age Social Movement* (Detroit, 2000) 83, 86, 173, 197(n.40). But the historical contingency of place never quite allowed that issue to blow up as much as race did. Besides the issue of labor, the determining factor of particular highlighted social issues, therefore, was not the Order itself, but other factors such as places of events and people who reacted strongly based on misunderstanding – but it was not the Knights, nor should it be historians.

[138] Letter, 8 October 1879, Powderly Papers, in *Black Worker*, 243.

But events would not allow labor to be the supreme issue. District Assembly 49, from New York, had one black man among its delegates to the national convention for the Knights of Labor held in Richmond in October 1886: Frank Ferrell, a unionist and socialist. When the group arrived in Richmond, a Southern city where racial segregation was already a matter of custom, and went to stay in their arranged lodging, the hotel's clerk realized that a black man was among the party and hence denied Ferrell admittance because of his race. "Without hesitation," according to Powderly's rendition, the delegates left the establishment.[139] The *Richmond Dispatch* defended the local norm, "This was in accordance with what had long been the custom here, and old customs and prejudices do not readily vanish."[140] But the *New York Freeman*, a black newspaper, praised the "49ers" (the delegates of District Assembly 49) for displaying "true manhood and most unusual courage" in "the simple matter of justice and fair play."[141] "Let the good work go on," it urged.[142]

---

[139] Terence Powderly, *Thirty Years of Labor, 1859-1889* (Columbus, Ohio, 1889), 652.
[140] *Richmond Dispatch* (Virginia), 5 October 1886, in *Black Worker*, 107.
[141] *New York Freeman*, 2 October 1886, in *Black Worker*, 105

However, the *New York Freeman* misunderstood the situation. Even the member of District 49 who was quoted in the article did not advance any racial agenda – although *New York Freeman* seemed to think so. As the 49er explained, "Every Knight of Labor, when he enters the order knows that his obligation makes him disregard the color, creed, and nationality of his fellow members." Clearly, race was not the only possible societal barrier to this Knight's brotherhood with other Knights. Moreover, he emphasized unity with fellow members rather than any proclivity to challenging the Southern racial norms. In fact, when "the colored delegate" Ferrell learned of the hotel's policy, he had "secured a place for himself, and said the other delegates could select any hotel they liked." However, the other delegates, "by a unanimous vote, declared they would only go where their colored brother was admitted on the same footing." They were not particularly interested in supporting black rights, but when the place they were staying highlighted a particular dividing line, they stood by as brothers in the Order, not as supporters of black rights or as objectors to social norms. In fact, they did not insist on being allowed to stay

[142] *Ibid.*, 106.

71

at that particular hotel against the social rules it followed: "The Assembly then looked about to devise a way out of the trouble. It finally sent the colored delegate and a white brother to Richmond to secure board for the entire delegation among colored families in that city."[143] They had not, as Melton Alonza McLaurin later claimed as a historian, "insisted upon equal treatment" for Ferrell.[144] Apparently unaware of the racial norms, they did not push against these norms of public accommodation at the hotel, but rather sought to avoid challenging the social customs. Still, by even trying at the hotel, the damage had already been done in the eyes of many white Southerners.

Nevertheless, the event that would cause the biggest uproar was still to come. While McLaurin thought that "Powderly chose Ferrell to introduce him,"[145] it was the Master Workman (the Knight leader of a particular district) of District Assembly 49, J.E. Quinn, who asked the General Master Workman (the leader of the entire Order) Powderly to include Ferrell in the opening of the

---

[143] *Ibid.*, 105.
[144] Melton Alonza McLaurin, *The Knights of Labor in the South* (Westport, Connecticut, 1978), 143.
[145] *Ibid.*

convention. Quinn had asked Powderly to allow Ferrell to introduce Virginia's Governor, Fitzhugh Lee, in the General Assembly of the Knights of Labor to open the national convention that would span most of the month. Powderly rejected the idea by telling Quinn, "I do not believe that it would be an act of courtesy on our part to violate any recognized rule of this community, and it would not be pleasant for either the Governor or the convention to attempt to set at defiance a long-established usage." Clearly, Powderly did not want to challenge the white South's social customs. Nevertheless, Powderly came to a compromise with Quinn: Ferrell would introduce Powderly, who would, in turn, introduce Governor Lee.[146]

On 4 October 1886, "the ablest exponent of the [Negro] race in the Knights of Labor circles," Frank Ferrell, in a brief address, formally introduced who he called "one of the noblest sons of labor," Terence Powderly, to the General Assembly of the Knights of Labor.[147] Ferrell tried to appeal to the pride of Virginians, declaring that Virginia

---

[146] Powderly, *Thirty Years of Labor*, 652-653.
[147] *The Freeman* (Indianapolis, IN), 8 February 1890, in *Black Worker*, 134; *Proceedings*, General Assembly, Knights of Labor, 1886, pp.7-8, in *Black Worker*, 106.

was "one of the oldest states in the avenue of political influence in our country" and hoping that just as it had "led in the aspirations of our country in the past," it would "lead in the future to the realization of the objects of the noble Order." One of those objects, Ferrell asserted, was the "abolition of these distinctions which are maintained by creed or color," and he praised Powderly as "a man above the superstitions which are involved in these distinctions."[148] While Ferrell's speech might seem inflammatory, the focus of the ensuing uproar was not the content of his speech, but rather the simple fact that a black man introduced a white man. Powderly stepped on stage and argued that education of the laborer, black and white, was necessary for future progress and prosperity. Both speeches argued for the advancement of labor without distinction between black or white. More importantly, a black man introducing a white man in the convention aggravated Southern social mores.

The agitation of white Southern sensibilities would continue during the opening days of the national

---

[148] *Proceedings*, General Assembly, Knights of Labor, 1886, pp.7-8, in *Black Worker*, 106.

convention. On 5 October, the 49ers went to a local theater and bought tickets in bulk to the evening's show. When Frank Ferrell sat in the orchestra rather than the gallery designated for a colored audience, "a few [whites] left the hall" and others offered "severe criticism of the management for allowing this violation of the long-established customs of this part of the country." The manager confessed that "he knew nothing of the presence of a negro until after his entrance into the hall," at which point he "thought it wiser and better for all concerned not to make any move which might possibly result in a disturbance."[149] But by no means had the white 49ers "helped him [Ferrell] to integrate a Richmond theater," as the historian Weir believed.[150] The next evening, attendance to that theater was "very slim" because of many who were "determined to boycott it." Even further, according to Powderly's retelling, outside the building, "an angry mob assembled, armed with revolvers and other weapons for the purpose of preventing one negro from entering the theatre."[151]

---

[149] *Richmond Dispatch* (Virginia), 6 October 1886, in *Black Worker*, 108.
[150] Weir, *Beyond Labor's Veil*, 49.
[151] Powderly, *Thirty Years of Labor*, 654-655.

Such a strong reaction by local whites to prevent any admittance was probably because the local whites thought the 49ers to be, as the *Richmond Dispatch* put it, "ready to make a 'test case'" on the issue of social equality between the races.[152] However, this was an erroneous judgment by the local whites, because there was evidence of the Northern delegates simply being unaware of the local customs. As Terence Powderly, a Pennsylvanian, wrote, "Until that time I did not know that colored men were denied admittance to theaters in this city."[153] Black people were not normally denied admittance into theaters, they were just segregated – but Powderly, being so unaware of the local customs, misunderstood the issue to be about admission. Still, most of the local whites did not see his naïve perspective; they understood the night at the theater as an open and direct challenge to Southern social norms.

In the aftermath of the incident, perhaps no person who wrote to Powderly understood the events in Richmond better than an individual from Washington,

---

[152] *Richmond Dispatch* (Virginia), 6 October 1886, in *Black Worker*, 108.
[153] Powderly, *Thirty Years of Labor*

D.C. He pointed out to Powderly that "both your wisdom and your courage have been subjected to a crucial test." The letter used the language of "human rights, irrespective of caste, religion, race or color," but it did so only within the context of "the interest of the working classes." As he told Powderly, "You stand more prominently than any man in the United States for the great producing classes."[154] In such a spotlight, a huge uproar ensued.

Was the Order, at its peak in 1886, trying to challenge the social customs of race relations in the South? With the incipient and growing industrialization of the New South in the late nineteenth century, the Order tried to bolster its growing Southern support by holding its national convention in Richmond, former capital of the Confederacy. When the Knights convened for the national convention, the Order allowed black people to attend, though in accordance with local customs, they sat segregated by race.[155] So what was the relationship between labor and race? Was the Order as an

---

[154] Letter, 6 October 1886, Terence Powderly Papers, reel 18.
[155] Howard Rabinowitz, *Race Relations in the Urban South, 1865-1890* (Oxford University Press: New York, 1978), 70-71.

organization promoting what many whites Southerners feared as "social equality" between the races? People around the country questioned, as a college student in Pennsylvania entitled his essay, "The Knights of Labor – What they aim at?"[156]

Historians have often misunderstood this question. Woodward recognized a "democratic idealism" in the Order as an organization.[157] Leon Fink claimed, "The Knights loomed in the mid-1880s as a beacon of racial enlightenment in a dark sea. In no other contemporary organization, it appears, was there such a quickening dynamic toward, rather than away from, racial equality."[158] Perhaps that was what the those who reacted disapprovingly of the Richmond incidents mistakenly thought the Knights intended, but racial equality was certainly not what the Order as an organization espoused via its leadership. McLaurin was more specific about Powderly, arguing that he "held even more advanced views about race" than the previous General Master Workman Uriah Stephens. McLaurin

---

[156] Letter, 27 October 1886, Terence Powderly Papers, reel 19.
[157] Woodward, *Origins of the New South*, 229.
[158] Leon Fink, *Workingmen's Democracy: The Knights of Labor and American Politics* (Chicago, 1983), 169.

quoted Stephens, "in labor, there is no distinction of Race. We all stand or fall together." This sounded exactly like Powderly's view on race – not "more advanced" than Stephens.[159] Neither Powderly nor the Order's platform held any particular "commitment to racial equality" as Weir interpreted it.[160]

In reality, these events in Richmond demonstrated that the Knights of Labor, the only national labor organization of its time was not radical because of its inclusion of black workers; it was strictly a labor organization whose leadership was not specifically interested in advancing rights for black people. The Noble Order of the Knights of Labor, the nation's first interracial labor union was not fighting for social equality between blacks and whites, but rather it was fighting for labor. This labor organization admitted blacks only so that labor may have solidarity in its own movement, but it did not strive for racial equality in society at large. The Knights of Labor were not struggling on behalf of blacks; they were struggling solely on behalf of labor.

---

[159] McLaurin, *The Knights of Labor in the South*, 132.
[160] Weir, *Beyond Labor's Veil*, 46.

The main reason those who disapproved of the Richmond incidents feared the specter of racial equality supposedly promoted by the Knights of Labor was because of the bugaboo of so-called "social equality" in the South. As the historian Daniel Letwin explained, "However vague in the abstract, the racial thrust of the 'social equality' charge was lost on no southerner."[161] Ralph Ellison, in his novel written from the perspective of a black man living in Southern society, illustrated just what a reaction "social equality" received by white Southerners when he wrote about the young man's early encounter with mistakenly using that familiar term in an unthinking moment distracted by blood in his mouth under pressure to yell "social responsibility" repeatedly to the white crowd:

> The room filled with the uproar of laughter until, no doubt, distracted by having to gulp down my

[161] Daniel Letwin, *The Challenge of Interracial Unionism: Alabama Coal Miners, 1878-1921* (Chapel Hill, 1998) 82. Letwin grasped the importance of the term "social equality" and its implications in labor, including for the Knights. He understood, "Challenging all norms of southern race relations had never been a part of the Knights' agenda; many, especially whites, would have found such an endeavor personally unpalatable, and all would have viewed it as politically suicidal" (pp.82-83).

blood, I made a mistake and yelled a phrase I had often seen denounced in newspaper editorials, heard debated in private.

"Social . . ."

"What?" they yelled.

". . . equality –"

The laughter hung smokelike in the sudden stillness. I opened my eyes, puzzled. Sounds of displeasure filled the room. The M.C. rushed forward. They shouted hostile phrases at me. But I did not understand.

A small dry mustached man in the front row blared out, "Say that slowly, son!"

"What, sir?"

"What you just said!"

"Social responsibility, sir," I said.

"You weren't being smart, were you, boy?" he said, not unkindly.

"No, sir!"

81

"You sure that about 'equality' was a mistake?"

"Oh, yes, sir," I said. "I was swallowing blood."

"Well, you had better speak more slowly so we can understand. We mean to do right by you, but you've got to know your place at all times. All right, now, go on with your speech."[162]

Although the particulars of what "social equality" meant were vague (it could include, for example, the Richmond incidents, but it was certainly not limited to those types of occurrences), the end result remained clear to most white Southerners: "Social equality means miscegenation," as one South Carolina newspaper proclaimed.[163] But the Knights did not promote "social equality" – the problem was the paranoid confusion by so many white Southerners. George Washington Cable, a former Confederate cavalryman who later supported

[162] Ralph Ellison, *Invisible Man* (New York, 1947, republished 1982), 25.
[163] *Charleston News and Courier*, quoted, McLaurin, *The Knights of Labor in the South*, 144.

"civil equality" but not "social equality" explained the problem in 1890 in a section of The Negro Question entitled "Distinction Between Civil and Social Equality": "The mere ambiguity of a term here has cost much loss. The double meaning of the words 'social' and 'society' seems to have been a real drawback on the progress of political ideas among the white people of the South. The clear and definite term, civil equality, they have made synonymous with the very vague and indefinite term, social equality, and then turned and totally misapplied it to the sacred domains of private society."[164] This white Louisianan believed that "Americans, in general, [i.e. people that were not white Southerners, such as Powderly in this case]" understood "that public society – civil society – comprises one distinct group of mutual relations, and private society entirely another, and that it is simply and only evil to confuse the two."[165] That

[164] George Washington Cable, *The Negro Question* (New York, 1890, republished 1903), 43-44.

[165] *Ibid.*, 44. Cable did attempt to explain, but not justify, to "Northern minds [that] are often puzzled to know why the whites of our Southern States, almost alone, should be beset by a confusion of ideas that costs them all the tremendous differences, spiritual and material, between a state of truce and a state of peace." He pointed to slavery: "Slavery was both public and private, domestic as well as civil... The defensive line of private society in its upper ranks was an attenuated one; hence

confused understanding by most white Southerners was precisely what led to the uproar around the Richmond incidents; it was what caused the conflict between Powderly's insistence on the distinction similar to that of Cable's and white Southern rejection of that explanation. So, then, how did the Knights of Labor draw this distinction? How did it stand so firmly for labor only?

In a sense, the Order followed the advice of Frederick Douglass, when he addressed the National Convention of Colored Men in Kentucky just three years earlier. Douglass called his audience's "earnest attention" to "the condition of the laboring class at the South." He recommended, "The labor unions of the country should not throw away this colored element of strength." At this particular historical moment, Douglass prioritized labor over race: "Today no subject wears an aspect more threatening to civilization than the respective claims of capital and labor, landlords and tenants." Like Booker T. Washington, Douglass understood racial issues within the

---

there was a constant, well-grounded fear that social confusion – for we may cast aside the term 'social equality' as preposterous – that social confusion would be wrought by the powerful temptation of close and continual contact between two class." But he believed such fear was no longer useful after slavery (pp.44-46).

larger context of labor. He continued in his address to advocate the solidarity of labor, "It is a great mistake for any class of laborers to isolate itself and thus weaken the bond of brotherhood between those on whom the burden and hardships of labor fall."[166]

Thus it comes as no surprise that Douglass' son, Charles Douglass, wrote to Powderly during the commotion surrounding the events of the 1886 convention. Powderly had written a public letter just days after the uproar about allowing a black man to introduce him. In this letter, Powderly stated, "I have no wish to interfere with the social relations which exist between the races of the South." Rather, he insisted, what he advocated was that "Southern cheap labor, regardless of color, must learn to read and write... [because it was such] a menace to the American toiler." He made explicitly clear that "the time-honored laws of social equality will be allowed to slumber undisturbed."[167] Yet, Charles Douglass nonetheless approved: "Your sentiments

---

[166] Frederick Douglass, Proceedings, National Convention of Colored Men at Louisville, Kentucky, 24 September 1883, in *Black Worker*, 35.

[167] Terence Powderly, *Richmond Dispatch*, 12 October 1886, in *Black Worker*, 107.

as expressed in your letter to the public... regarding the color question, and more especially the social aspect of the case, deserves and will receive the highest commendation by the colored people throughout the length and breadth of this country." He told Powderly that he would forward the letter to his father, Frederick Douglass, who was visiting Europe. He was confident that his father "will awaken in his breast grateful emotions towards you, and the order you so graciously preside over and represent."[168] Powderly was not calling for social equality between the races. Powderly's stance was clear and unchallenging. By falling in line with Booker T. Washington, it did not contradict even a staunch advocate like Frederick Douglass, who seemed to find the issue of labor supreme as well. There were no illusions.

Those who misunderstood Powderly's action as advocating social equality were mainly white Southerners, especially in Richmond. With the perceived attacks on Southern social customs, the *Richmond Dispatch* began to dig for other news that would indirectly show the supposed stance of the Order toward social equality

---

[168] Letter, 12 October 1886, Terence Powderly Papers, reel 19.

between the blacks and whites. For example, a reporter went into a hotel and confirmed the rumor that a white delegate to the General Assembly was sleeping in the same bed as a black man (not a delegate). "The conversation ended here, and the reporter left," stated the *Richmond Dispatch*. Obviously, the sole fact that the reporter wished to know was whether or not a black man and a white man slept together in the same bed – a major sin in a South that was on the verge of mandating segregation by law – demonstrating just how important it was to know the fact he uncovered. In that same issue, the newspaper reported that a black delegate from Baltimore was receiving the same treatment as the white guests in his hotel – this was unacceptable within the customs of segregation developing in the South. Apparently, as soon as the hotel proprietor found out, he told the white delegates that "the negro could not be given the first-class accommodations."[169]

The *Richmond Dispatch* went further with its wariness and suspicion of the Knights of Labor. The next day, it described the black delegate from Baltimore as

---

[169] *Richmond Dispatch* (Virginia), 6 October 1886, in *Black Worker*, 108.

"quite a black negro," thus defining the man not only by his race, but by the shade of his color, thereby showing that not only did race itself play a role in the perception of a person but so did the very degree of color. In the same issue, the *Richmond Dispatch* reported that four white delegates of the General Assembly got in a streetcar with a black woman. It also mentioned that three other white delegates got into a carriage with two black women, "one very black and one yellow."[170] Again, the newspaper was judging the black women by the hue of their color. But the more important implication of this newsworthy story is its clear fear of the mixing of the races, which the emergent social rules of segregation in the South strictly prohibited. Miscegenation was perhaps the worst form of race mixing, since its very implication was that of social equality between the races. By diluting the purity of each race, one was undermining the very distinction of his race from the other, thereby admitting racial equality. Miscegenation was the ultimate sin in promoting racial equality – and the *Richmond Dispatch* was suspiciously examining the Knights for evidence of that crime.

---

[170] *Richmond Dispatch* (Virginia), 7 October 1886, in *Black Worker*, 113.

The fact that these pieces of information were newsworthy shows the social customs of racial relations in Richmond. It was the violation of these customs of separation in social relations, especially in public (theater, hotel, streetcar, introduction), that white Southerners understood as among the incidents implying social equality. It was not the violations of particular governmental laws. Even outside the South, the *Chicago Herald* recognized that the uproar was due to "local customs and prejudice," which it mentioned seven times in the same article – and expressed its disapproval of those local customs.[171] In Virginia, one newspaper pointed toward the prominence of these customs. In referring to the "peculiar and offensive notions of social equality" about hotel accommodations held by the Knights of District 49, the newspaper reported, "We have heard some worthy people argue that such equality was repulsive simply by reason of custom." The newspaper disagreed, but still did not recognize governmental laws of segregation: "The distinctions between the two races are fixed, we believe, by a higher law than human statutes, and will continue for all time."[172] Thus the

---

[171] *Chicago Herald*, 7 October 1886, Powderly Papers, reel 18.

Knights did not break any segregation laws, which had not yet become statutes, but many Southern whites did indeed believe the Knights violated social customs.

The *Richmond Dispatch* published explicit local reactions that were disapproving of the actions of the Knights of District 49. It quoted one of the most prominent Knights of Richmond as condemning his fellow Knights' actions as an "outrage upon the people of this city, and an insult to the Knights of Labor of the United States." Referring to the Knights from Richmond, he pointed out that "their position of host only restrains them from an outburst of righteous contempt." He further warned, "The action of 49 will cause a great many to leave the order."[173] He claimed that he had not met anybody, black or white, who did not have the "severest condemnation" of the 49ers. He declared that he could not find "anything [the United States Constitution and the by-laws of the Knights included] upon which 49 can lay any claim for social equality." He thought the only

---

[172] *Norfolk Virginian*, 30 October 1886, in *Black Worker*, 133.
[173] The membership in the Knights of Labor dropped from seven-hundred-thousand in 1886 to one-hundred-thousand in 1890, but it is not clear how much of that was due to issues of race raised by this incident – 1886 was also the year of the Haymarket Riot.

possibility would be through the Declaration of Independence ("All men are created equal."), but "people may accept as much of the doctrine as thy please; as for myself, I do not in any way accept it as a fact."[174] This was an example of a perception of social equality from slavery to civil rights: the Constitution was not seen as a doctrine for social equality and the Declaration of Independence was only partially accepted. But more specifically to the case at hand, this Richmond Knight demonstrated that despite the doctrine of the Knights extending across racial lines, it went only so far as equality within the labor movement, but certainly not social equality. Even though Powderly would agree, many Southern whites, including this member of the Order, viewed the actions by the Knights of District 49 at the hotel and theater not as a brotherhood in labor but as promoting social equality.

Not all the local reaction to the Knights of Labor was negative: one white Virginia Knight understood the situation perfectly. Supportive of the actions of the General Assembly, he declared, "A colored Knight of Labor must be placed on equal terms with a Knight of

---

[174] *Richmond Dispatch* (Virginia), 7 October 1886, in *Black Worker*, 109.

Labor who is white, so far as wages and political rights are concerned."[175] This white Virginian fully understood that the Knights were advocating equal rights between the races only in labor and politics (in order to vote as labor) – this was precisely what Powderly would advocate days later in the public letter. As the Order's official newspaper had stated years earlier when recruiting black workers, "We should be false to every principle of our Order should we exclude from membership any man who gains his living by honest toil, on account of his color or creed."[176] The Order had made its purpose of black recruitment clear through an official resolution when meeting in Washington, D.C. in 1884, "Resolved, That the efforts of all working men and women should first be devoted to the compact, thorough organization of all trades or callings whatsoever, regardless of sex, creed or color, with the single purpose of elevating and protecting labor, and to this end ceaseless agitation and education must be conducted."[177] The Knights were fighting for the laboring

---

[175] Letter, *New York Tribune* (New York), 10 October 1886, in *Black Worker*, 116.
[176] *Journal of United Labor*, 15 August 1880, in *Black Worker*, 72.
[177] *National Republican* (Washington, D.C.) 5 February 1884, in *Black Worker*, 72.

class as a whole, which included blacks and whites; but they were not fighting for the advancement solely of blacks. The aforementioned Virginia Knight did not worry about the perception of social equality being promoted by the Order, unlike many of his fellow white Southerners, because he realized the organization was not fighting for social equality.[178]

Still, without a doubt, the local contempt against the perceived promotion of social equality by the Knights of Labor was no small voice – it was even covered by the mainstream national press. One Richmond Knight fumed to the *New York Times*, "We have white and colored Knights of Labor here, and they are members of different assemblies. A colored man has all the rights of a white man here except socially. They are satisfied with things as they are, and it is not right for you to come here and tear

---

[178] Although this white Knight's approval of Powderly contradicts McLaurin's claim, McLaurin is right as a generalization that most white Southern members "refused to accept the more liberal views of the order's leadership" (*Knights*, p.144). More accurately, though, McLaurin should recognize that it was only a perception by these whites that the leadership was any more liberal on race than they were – a perception driven by the specter of social equality, which Powderly (from outside the South) did not comprehend the intricacies.

us all to pieces." He warned that acting against these customs of social relations between the races would "break up the Knights of Labor here." Another Richmond Knight supported that statement, "The forcing of a colored man among white people here has knocked me out of the order."[179] Clearly, the Southern Knights did not perceive the Knights of Labor as an organization for promoting social equality. The *New York Times* assessed the local situation, "The order will never attain any considerable strength among the white population of the South" because it had made an "unpardonable mistake" that "aroused a storm of indignation."[180]

The *New York Times* was correct in its assessment: white Southerners, not just whites from Richmond, were angry at the Order. One white Southern Knight wrote to Terence Powderly in disbelief, "I cannot believe that our colored brothers will be set up by our General order as our social equals."[181] A white Alabamian informed Powderly, "There is only one way for you to find

179 *New York Times* (New York), 7 October 1886, in *Black Worker*, 110.
180 *Ibid.*, 109.
181 Letter, 6 October 1886, Terence Powderly Papers, in *Black Worker*, 114.

out what a nigger is, that is to come south and stay 3 months." First, he taught Powderly about the perceived laziness and ineptness of blacks, "In the north, Mr. Powderly, one white girl does all the work for a family of five or six people, while you have to hire 3 to do the same work. A colored girl that cooks won't wash, and one that washes won't do the house work." Then, he complained about the "smell [of blacks] when they get heated up that is sickening." Next, he compared the laboring class of the South against that of the North (having himself lived in both regions for a significant number of years), "I believe the laboring man here gets along better than in the north they have less clothes and fuel to buy." This argument echoed a major part of the pro-slavery argument in the antebellum South: the laboring class in the South (the slaves) had better material conditions than the laboring class in the North, at least in part due to low wages in the North often failing to provide to workers what the master provided to his slaves (i.e. food, clothing, shelter). Finally, the writer of the letter attempted to demonstrate the freedom of blacks by pointing out that in Montgomery, "The colored people have Fire and military companies, civic societies, and many other things of that kind here, and are never interfered with, and are treated just as good as any people in the north are treated."[182] He used these segregated institutions to argue autonomy of blacks.

The attacks on Powderly went beyond just arguments to insults against his person. A Texan wrote to Powderly: "Since you have changed from a Knight of Labor advocate to a nigger social equality man I hereby denounce you as a low, vulgar buffoon than whom there is none more contemptable." Clearly, this man did not see social equality as part of the Knights of Labor agenda, as shown by his comment about Powderly having "changed" from a Knight to a "nigger social equality man." He then let Powderly know that "a decent nigger should shun you," hence demonstrating his belief in the black docility and happiness with an inferior status. Finally, when the writer signed his name, he did so in the following manner: "James Hirst—now and henceforth an ex-Knight of Labor."[183] Obviously, Hirst's anger drove him away from the Knights (again proving correct the assessment by the

---

[182] Letter, 16 October 1886, in *Black Worker*, 115.
[183] Letter, 13 October 1886, Powderly Papers, in *Black Worker*, 114.

New York Times), despite the fact that he believed Powderly to have separated from the organization's ideals. Still, he recognized Powderly's commanding position as General Master Workman and hence his power to lead the organization, so he therefore disassociated with it in disgust and anticipation of future organizational endeavors.

Such disdainful attacks against Powderly were not limited only to men. One woman wrote to Powderly sardonically and succinctly: "Dear Sir: —As you are so much in sympathy with the negro, will you please call over and fill our coachmen's place until he gets well? Inquire on Church Hill."[184]

Disbelief also came from those within the Order who reside outside Virginia. One white Knight from Alabama enclosed a story from a newspaper reporting the incidents at the hotel and the theater with the Knights of District 49. He attached a letter to it, proclaiming, "I cannot believe that our colored brothers will be set up by our own grand order as our social equals." This white Knight was willing to ally with black workers on behalf of

---

[184] Powderly, *Thirty Years of Labor*, 660.

labor, but he did not want to challenge Southern racial customs. Thus, when he maintained, "We are willing to aid our colored brethren by all legitimate ways in the great fight for freedom," he had in mind the struggle for labor. When social customs were violated, "public sympathy" turned "emphatically against" the Order. He apologized for taking Powderly's time, but he felt so strongly that it was his he believes his "duty demands it as a local Knight, for such is the sentiment of my people."[185] Even this white Southern Knight, who disapproved of Powderly's actions, accepted black equality within the labor movement. Thus was not vehemently against any interaction with black people altogether, but rather he wished that equality to remain within the context of labor, for the sake of labor. Despite Powderly's concurrence, the perceived disagreement came over actions with regard to social customs, such as at the theater and hotel, and hence what they deemed social equality.

Not all the letters to Powderly misunderstood the situation. One person from Alabama wrote a letter that

---

[185] Letter, 6 October 1886, Powderly Papers, reel 18.

merely said, "I can not refrain from stating just a word of approval of your course and words in relation to the rights of the Negro – it is not a question of social equality."[186] With the letter dated after Powderly's public letter, the author of this letter might have already read Powderly's explicit statements. Regardless, he understood the distinctions of equality and the fact that the Order did not wish to promote social equality.

Beyond people writing letters, the white Southern press also reacted strongly through articles and editorials against Powderly and the Knights of Labor for allegedly promoting social equality between the races. A Georgia newspaper questioned whether it was "the purpose of the Knights of Labor to settle social as well as labor questions."[187] Clearly, there was a conscious distinction between labor issues and social issues, yet many newspapers amidst their fear and frenzy did not acknowledge that the Knights of Labor also made this distinction. Thus, another Georgia newspaper fretted and warned, "Social intermixture is the first and longest step

---

[186] Letter, 13 October 1886, Powderly Papers, reel 19.
[187] *Savannah News* (Georgia), 8 October 1886, in *Black Worker*, 111.

toward miscegenation, which means mongrelization."[188] Here again, was the fear of racial mixture and consequently racial equality. A North Carolina newspaper sharply notified its readers, "It is well that our people should be warned in time of the news and vile use to which the Knights of Labor organization is to be put—that is to say, if the Southern Knights will consent thus to be used."[189] As it turned out, the Southern Knights did indeed end up taking official action in the form of a resolution.

Some Northern papers had an answer to these negative white Southern reactions. Upon learning that the "aristocratic workingmen of Richmond" were "disgusted" and threatened withdrawal from the Knights of Labor, a Philadelphia newspaper indignantly wrote, "They had better withdraw and stay out until they learn that honest labor ennobles every doer on the face of the green earth."[190] It's worth noting that it did not refer to a general social equality between races but merely to labor.

---

[188] *August News* (Georgia), 9 October 1886, in *Black Worker*, 112.

[189] *Raleigh News and Observer*, 7 October 1886, in *Black Worker*, 111.

[190] *North American* (Philadelphia, Pennsylvania), 7 October 1886, in *Black Worker*, 111.

A newspaper out of Harrisburg held the same limitations on equality, "The workingmen of this country know no color line. They stand shoulder to shoulder."[191] It did not make mention about equality in society, but rather equality among those who labor for the sake of solidarity. "Laboring men struggling to better their condition have a common cause which binds them together in a common brotherhood. There can be no color line,"[192] declared another Philadelphia newspaper. The context of the racial equality was only among "laboring men," not among the men (and women) of society. This perception was in-line with that of the Order: it fought solely for the rights of labor (which included blacks), not for the rights of race.

Besides the press, outside the South, Powderly also received commentary through letters, including a few from high profile individuals. Robert Blissert, head of New York City's Central Labor Union, expressed his "pride and gratitude." With regard to the Knights of District 49, Powderly "was manly and Christian like and cannot fail but to enlist the sympathy of our enemies. It was the

---

[191] *Telegraph* (Harrisburg, Pennsylvania), 5 October 1886, in *Black Worker*, 111.
[192] *Press* (Philadelphia, Pennsylvania), 8 October 1886, in *Black Worker*, 111.

language of a free American."[193] From The Gilman House in Portland, Oregon, came assurance of "the colored citizens of the far northwest as your most devoted friends."[194] Samuel Pomeroy, former U.S. Senator from Kansas, approved of Powderly's public letter "upon the color question as it bears upon the labor question." In agreement with Powderly's espousal, Pomeroy argued, "One laborer depressed and oppressed is a weight upon all." He applauded Powderly's efforts to "uplift the poor colored laborer," but only within the context of labor uplift, not black racial uplift.[195]

Despite the lack of support for black social uplift within the Order, black sentiment around the country was supportive of the labor organization. While the actions during the General Assembly of 1886 drove some white people away from the Knights, it drew more black people toward it. The all-black Local Assembly 1935 (in Ohio) of the Knights of Labor passed a resolution to "renew our obligations to the Order and pledge ourselves to do all in power to swell the number of our ranks, and declare that

[193] Letter, 5 October 1886, Powderly Papers, reel 18.
[194] Letter, 15 October 1886, Powderly Papers, reel 19.
[195] Letter, 12 October 1886, Powderly Papers, reel 19.

we will never relinquish our work until the bulk of our brethren in city, town, County and State are brought within the folds of our noble Order."[196] Similarly, one labor newspaper published a letter from a black Knight. In this letter, the black Knight emphasized that "colored men would be recognized in the K. of L." As he urged, "I will say to my people, Help the cause of labor."[197] Another person wrote to Powderly from Alabama, "There are a great many desiring a lodge both white and colored."[198] These black Knights felt rejuvenated and reenergized after the events of the General Assembly.

Black people around the country wrote letters to Powderly. From Jacksonville, Florida, came a letter "to congratulate" Powderly "in the behalf of my race" about the his public letter, which supported black equality within labor, but clearly denounced social equality between the races.[199] A black person from Maryland appreciated "the rebuke" Powderly's public letter "gave the narrow minded men of the Southern press." As he

---

[196] *Cleveland Gazette* (Ohio), 13 November 1886, in *Black Worker*, 126.

[197] Letter, *John Swinton's Paper*, 10 October 1886, in *Black Worker*, 76.

[198] Letter, 25 October 1886, Powderly Papers, reel 19.

[199] Letter, 12 October 1886, Powderly Papers, reel 19.

continued, "The colored citizens of the state of Maryland unanimously tender you their heartfelt thanks for having assumed such a manly position in defense of an oppressed people."[200] Despite Powderly's position on social equality, presumably the letter was approving his defense of black equality within labor. This represents a position that did not advocate for civil rights, but one similar to that of Booker T. Washington, who pushed for industrial education and equality in work. As a committee on behalf of a black photography business, Goodridge Brothers, in Michigan wrote Powderly: "We feel that you have the sympathy and approbation of seven millions of patient, peaceful colored laborers with twelve hundred thousand loyal votes, in your efforts to give equal and exact justice to all of its citizens, under and through the laws of our country."[201] The letter not only recognized equal rights within the context of labor, but it also did not challenge the laws. Once again, the focus was on industrial equality.

Perhaps none of the letters Powderly received from black Americans were as candid as one from the

---

[200] Letter, 13 October 1886, Powderly Papers, reel 19.
[201] Letter, 19 October 1886, Powderly Papers, reel 19.

nation's capital. After identifying himself as a "colored citizen," the writer thanked Powderly for his "noble stand" in Richmond. He pointed to the "outrageous treatment to which we [black people] are daily subjected by the white people of the South." He explained that "we have been patient under trying circumstances... We protected their women and children and fed and clothed their old men and in no instance was the trust betrayed." The writer also stressed the injustice in the application of the law, although not referring to any actual statute, "No man is silly enough to believe that a white man will be punished for the murder of a colored man in the South." He called the reader's attention to black Americans' service to the country: "We have given two hundred and fifty years of our labor to the material advancement of this country and yet we find court and jury combined against us, while even handed justice is meted out to the humblest foreigners." In spite of so many complaints, this black writer also stated, "Equality before the law is all we want and that does not mean social equality by any means."[202] This sounds similar to Powderly's call for equality before the law so labor can vote together, but

---

[202] Letter, 13 October 1886, Powderly Papers, reel 19.

they did not call for social equality in places such as theaters and hotels.

The Knights of Labor had made their intentions clear with a resolution during the General Assembly: "*Resolved*, That the Order of the Knights of Labor recognize the civil and political equality of all men and in the broad field of labor recognize no distinction on account of color, but it has no purpose to interfere with or disrupt the social relations which may exist between the different races in various portions of the country." This was a resolution that was introduced by W.H. Barrett of Philadelphia on behalf of the Southern Knights. With the passing of the resolution in the General Assembly, it was apparent that the Order officially agreed to not advocate social equality. This demonstrated the fact that the Knights never intended to challenge Southern customs to promote social equality between the races. "This action has had a soothing effect upon the Southern Knights," reported the *New York Times*.[203]

---

[203] *New York Times* (New York), 16 October 1886, in *Black Worker*, 129.

Still, on 19 October 1886, Powderly received a telegram from Little Rock, Arkansas, stating the following: "The negro press association now in session hail with joy the dispatches of the morning containing action of Knights of Labor convention now in session at Richmond in adopting resolution in regard to admission of colored apprentices in workshops and factories of the country on Equal footing with white apprentices."[204] The Knights of Labor was working toward racial equality only within the labor movement. The press association, in its telegram, mentioned nothing about social equality of blacks, but it mentioned equality within labor only. Despite knowing that the resolution explicitly stated that the Order did not advocate social equality between the races, the black press reacted positively to the labor organization's recognition of equality strictly within labor.

The black press expressed its excitement and approval, not only through the committee but in print as well. The *New York Freeman* felt that the Knights of Labor "took Southern prejudice, arrogance and intolerance by the throat and gave it the most furious shaking it has had

---

[204] Telegram, Negro Press Committee to Terence Powderly, 19 October 1886, in *Black Worker*, 115.

since the war." It was delighted that there was "one great organization in the land which recognizes the brotherhood of all men and has the courage to practice what it teaches."[205] The *New York Freeman* overstated the case, perhaps too quickly jumping to the assumption that the Knights supported social equality even outside of labor.

The *New York Freeman* had been closely following the question of race in labor before the Richmond events. Earlier in the year, the black newspaper declared, "We have taken the position that the colored laborers of the United States cannot afford to antagonize white laborers."[206] As the national convention of the Order approached, the newspaper argued, "A Knight of Labor is a Knight of Labor, be he black or white."[207]

Hence, after the racket, *New York Freeman* printed a sample of the different reactions among the black press of the time – while the convention in

---

[205] *New York Freeman* (New York), 9 October 1886, in *Black Worker*, 113.
[206] *New York Freeman* (New York), 22 May 1886, in *Black Worker*, 44.
[207] *New York Freeman* (New York), 2 October 1886, in *Black Worker*, 45.

Richmond continued. The Wilmington (North Carolina) *Chronicle* was pleased that the Knights of Labor had "shown itself courageous enough to face a strong popular prejudice and honest enough to stand up to one of its cardinal principles." The Petersburg (Virginia) *Lancet* surmised, "This certainly is a boom for the order among the colored people." The Salisbury (North Carolina) *Star of Zion* boldly stated, "They [the Knights of Labor] are doing more to blot out color prejudice and recognize the equality of manhood in all races than any organization in existence." Perhaps the Knights were doing more for race than any organization in 1886, but unlike the impression of the *Star of Zion*, it was not on behalf of blacks, but on behalf of labor. The Detroit (Michigan) *Plaindealer* also overstated the case, calling it "the most potent factor ever yet entered into our American life to secure full justice to the Afro-American." The Philadelphia (Pennsylvania) *Tribune* held perhaps the best understanding of the extent of racial equality promoted by the Knights of Labor. It concluded, "Though the leading spirits of the organization are full of hope and activity, and though they are inspired by the most proper sense of justice, it is doubtful that the rank and file of the order are ready to preach and practice industrial equality."[208] Indeed, the *Tribune* accurately recognized that the issue at hand was merely "industrial equality." Furthermore, it was sensible in realizing that, despite the aspirations set forth by the leaders of the organization, in practice, those aspirations would not often be realized – industrial equality could lead to social equality.

The *New York Freeman*, a newspaper so passionate about black rights was understandably disappointed by the Order's resolution passed later in the Richmond convention that explicitly rejected the promotion of social equality between the races. After initially lauding the Knights, the *New York Freeman* became frustrated. It lamented, "The North has never proved itself a match for the South." The newspaper referred to the Supreme Court decision of *Scott v. Sandford* (commonly known as the Dred Scott Decision) and also to the failure of Reconstruction in order to show why it was not "surprised" about the most recent case of Southern triumph.[209]

---

[208] *New York Freeman* (New York), 16 October 1886, in *Black Worker*, 129-131.

[209] *New York Freeman* (New York), 23 October 1886, in *Black Worker*, 132.

Notwithstanding the *New York Freeman*'s uncommon reaction, it became unmistakably clear that black leaders were not asking for the social equality that so many white Southerners feared, despite all the upheaval that erupted in Richmond. To show their gratitude for the impact of District Assembly 49 (Frank Ferrell at the hotel, Frank Ferrell introducing Terence Powderly, and Frank Ferrell entering the theater) on the city, Richmond blacks held a banquet for the 49ers. The *Pittsburgh Dispatch* reported, "All of these speakers disclaimed any desire on the part of the colored race to compel recognition as social equals." For example, in his welcome address, Colonel Wilson (a mulatto) plainly stated, in line with the accommodationist philosophy of Booker T. Washington, "We seek no change in the social customs... Our aim is not to establish a new social order of things for the people among whom we live."[210] Though the 49ers had unintentionally challenged the white South's social customs, it is clear that the local blacks of Richmond and even the defiant Knights of District Assembly 49 did not intend to promote social equality

---

[210] *Pittsburgh Dispatch* (Pennsylvania), 15 October 1886, in *Black Worker*, 128.

between the races, especially in the South. They were striving for equality in labor, thereby creating a unified labor movement.

This was exactly what Powderly advocated. On 11 October 1886, Powderly wrote a statement that the *Richmond Dispatch* published the next day. In it, he confirmed that it was his decision to have Frank Ferrell introduce him in the General Assembly. "I have not seen or heard an argument since then that would cause me to do differently to-day," he declared. He emphatically upheld his decision to have a black man (Ferrell) introduce a white man (Powderly himself). Then, he condemned "the hasty and inconsiderate action of those who were so quick to see an insult where none was intended." This meant that he did not mean to challenge the Southern customs on social equality between the races; it only seemed so because of the quick conclusions of others. Powderly knew that it would be an "insult" to Richmond to promote social equality between the races, so when he stated that "none was intended," it meant that he was not trying to break the local social mores. The shrill Southern press and apprehensive Southern whites had misconstrued his actions.[211]

Powderly attempted to justify his choice of Ferrell to introduce him. "Critics have seen fit to decide what I meant by selecting this man to introduce me, and they have asserted that my action must be regarded in the light of an attack upon the laws of social equality."[212] Instead, he explained, "My sole object in selecting a colored man to introduce me was to encourage and help to uplift his race from a bondage worse than that which held him in chains twenty-five years ago—viz.: mental slavery." This referred to the thoughts embodied in the speech he gave at the General Assembly about the importance of education to uplift the laboring class, black or white. Powderly continued, "I desired to impress upon the minds of white and black that the same result followed action in the field of labor, whether that action was on the part of the Caucasian or the Negro." Powderly thought it an appropriate illustration of his point on the importance of education by likening the ignorance of the laboring class in 1886 to the ignorance of at least part of the laboring class (slaves) before the Civil War. "I did not refer to social equality," Powderly avowed, "for that

---

[211] Powderly, *Thirty Years of Labor*, 656.
[212] *Ibid.*

cannot be regulated by law."[213] Powderly had referred to the education of the laboring class, black and white, since they were both a part of the laboring class and he championed the rights of labor. Powderly neither espoused the cause of social equality between the races nor thought it even possible to do so by law – therefore, he had no motivation in the first place to even try to push social equality between the races upon Southerners. So his intended message in the General Assembly certainly must not have been social equality.

Powderly made clear what types of customs with which he would not interfere – showing what he thought social equality was. After claiming that the law could not regulate social equality, he pointed out, "The sanctity of the fireside circle can not be invaded by those who are not welcome. Every man has the right to say who shall enter beneath his roof' who shall occupy the same bed, private conveyance, or such other place as he is master of. I reserve for myself the right to say who I will or will not associate with. That right belongs to every other man. I have no wish to interfere with that right."[214]

---

[213] *Ibid.*, 657.
[214] *Ibid.*

Powderly had "no wish to interfere with the social relations which exist[ed] between the races of the South," but he did have "a strong desire to see the black man educated" only because "Southern labor, regardless of color, must learn to read and write." He did not want to see the black man educated to elevate the race to the status of whites and thereby encourage social equality, nor did call for education of blacks but not whites. He aimed to educate *labor*, black or white, in order to advance *labor*. Powderly asked rhetorically, "Will my critics show me how the laws of social equality will be harmed by educating the black man so that he may know how to conduct himself as a gentleman? Will they explain how a knowledge of the laws of his country will cause a man to violate the laws of social equality."[215] In these questions, Powderly had implicitly accepted the customs regarding social equality already in place; he did not try to change, or even question, the so-called laws of social equality that were observed by society. In fact, the underlying suggestion behind those questions was that the black man be educated so that he would better follow those social customs.

---

[215] *Ibid.*, 658.

Powderly pointed to precedent to justify his actions as respectful of the racial social customs in the South. He asked, "Will my critics stop long enough to tell me why the United States Senate allowed a colored man to *introduce*, before the Vice-President of the United States, measures for the benefit of his state? Were the laws of social equality outraged when the House of Representatives permitted colored men to take seats in it? Why did not other southern representatives leave and return to their homes when that was done?"[216]

Powderly assured readers that "the time-honored laws of social equality will be allowed to slumber on undisturbed."[217] He articulated his requests, on behalf of the Knights of Labor, "The equality of American citizenship is all that we insist on, and that equality *must* not, *will* not, be trampled upon."[218] Here, he demanded "citizenship" rights for blacks because they were a part of the laboring class, and therefore their political power would help the labor movement's political power. It was not that Powderly purported black political rights for the

---

[216] *Ibid.*
[217] *Ibid.*
[218] *Ibid.*, 659.

sake of black Americans, but instead for the sake of labor. A black laborer's vote (an issue of *political* equality) was important to advance the labor movement, but a black laborer being unable to enter a theater or other private establishment on equal terms as whites (an issue of *social* equality) did not affect the labor movement. Thus, Powderly cared about the former but not the latter – the political equality but not the social equality.

Powderly reiterated: "In the field of labor and American citizenship we [the Knights] recognize no line of race, creed, politics or color." Again, Powderly advocated labor rights and political rights (which led to labor empowerment) for both blacks and whites. He did not include the question of broader social equality in that statement because he did not support social equality between the races. As he explicitly asserted, "The intelligent, educated man is better qualified to discern the difference between right and privilege, and the unwritten law of social equality will be more rigidly observed than it is to-day."[219] That statement demonstrates Powderly's unambiguous support of the contemporary customs

---

[219] *Ibid.*

regarding social equality – in fact, his support for increased sternness. Education was imperative, because understanding the difference between right and privilege was crucial; and that was important in order to understand and obey the laws of social equality, since they were unwritten. Powderly certainly never questioned the laws of social equality, but rather he shamelessly espoused them by promoting education for the exact reason that the laws of social equality be better upheld. In his mind, Powderly posed no threat whatsoever toward the so-called laws of social equality in Richmond during the 1886 General Assembly.

The *New York Freeman* was disappointed that Powderly "pandered his honest convictions" and "endeavored to soften and gloss over the matter in craven deference to the yell of the Southern white press and the demands of white Southern Knights of Labor."[220] But the *New York Freeman* had always overstated Powderly's convictions on the extent of racial equality. It was wrong to believe that Powderly had wavered from his

---

[220] *New York Freeman* (New York), 30 October 1886, in *Black Worker*, 133.

"honest convictions" since he had never argued for social equality in the first place.

Powderly had demonstrated his willingness to work within Southern social customs on race when he had talked about organizing black workers. As he had written in a letter to a Knight in Nashville, Tennessee, three years before the Richmond convention: "I think it the most prominent plan to organize them [black workers] in assemblies of their own."[221] Almost a year after the Richmond convention, after the uproar had subsided, Powderly again wrote that black workers "may be admitted to Assemblies having white members, but the best way is to organize them in Assemblies of their own and allow the work of education to do away with the prejudice now existing against them."[222] He wanted to organize black workers for labor solidarity, but to do so

---

[221] Letter, 1 October 1883, Powderly Papers, in *Black Worker*, 246.

[222] Letter, 19 July 1887, Powderly Papers, in *Black Worker*, 260. It's worth noting that McLaurin uses the same quote to show how "practical" Powderly was in his organization of labor and that this showed his "willingness to compromise" (*Knights*, p.133). But McLaurin earlier seems to believe the opposite when pointing out the support of segregated assemblies by Stephens (p.132). Therefore, applying the same standard, Powderly does not seem any "more advanced" than Stephens in his views on race, despite McLaurin's claim (p.132).

within the racially segregated social norms of the South because he believed such segregation did not hinder the organization's objective.

Years after the Richmond convention and its subsequent reactions, with the Order declining, Powderly wrote a book about his career in labor. Still, Powderly justified his actions in 1886 the same way he had in the statement he released to the *Richmond Dispatch* on 12 October of that year. His main validation of those actions was through the reprinting of the letter itself in the book. In the book he then continued to explain his intentions during the national convention of 1886: "Violation of the rules of social equality formed no part of the thought or intensions of the General Master Workman [Powderly] when he selected Mr. Ferrell to introduce him to the General Assembly." He did not wish to alter the customs of social equality in the South, and he stressed that "as a factor in the field of production, he [the black man] stood the equal of all other men."[223] Powderly again emphasized the equality of the black man to the white man related only to labor. He was probably writing his

---

[223] Powderly, *Thirty Years of Labor*, 660.

honest convictions in the book, given that it was written a few years after the event and he had nobody to appease, contrary to what the *New York Freeman* had thought in October of 1886.

In the book, Powderly angrily attacked many of those who had attacked him: "Social equality is recognized in the South by many of those who prate the loudest against it. The slave-owners of long ago leveled the distinctions between the races, and some of their children and children's children honor the practice to the present day." He then clarified his statement with a strikingly direct and unabashed comment: "The best evidence of the insincerity and hypocrisy of the Southern aristocrat is written upon the half-white faces of the hundreds of thousands of young men and women in whose veins flow, in mingled current, the blood of the former slave and that of the best families of the South."[224] With his criticism, Powderly lodged charges of miscegenation against those very whites who spoke the loudest against it. His ire brought to the fore, not only his anger toward those who attacked him years earlier but

---

[224] *Ibid.*, 661-662.

rather that he felt quite passionately against the mixing of the races himself. He disapproved of miscegenation, the epitome of social equality between the races. Furthermore, Powderly warned, "Of the two races in the South at the present time, the negro is making the most energetic struggle for an education. If the whites would not fall behind in the race they must learn that moral worth, not wealth, is the true standard of individual and national greatness."[225] His statement suggested some sort of fear of the white race falling behind the black race; with his warning and through his efforts, he wanted to assure that the white race always remained supreme to the black race in obeying the so-called laws of social equality.

These were the ideas about race held by the General Master Workman of the Noble Order of the Knights of Labor who was attacked by many Southern whites for promoting social equality between the races by allowing a black man to introduce him. Besides, the organization he led was also being accused of such purportedly despicable acts. Yet, the fear was completely

---

[225] *Ibid.*, 662.

unfounded and was the result of paranoia and overreaction. Interracial unionism did not aim to promote social equality but to promote labor. For the labor movement to have a chance at success, it needed solidarity. Black people, as well as white people, made up the laboring class. Hence, for the labor movement to be unified, it had to include both black laborers and white laborers. The Order had realized this fact when it allowed blacks to join its labor organization. It certainly had not allowed black workers to join out of any sense of racial justice; it had allowed black workers to join for the sake of labor solidarity.

Terence Powderly, the leader of the nation's most prominent labor union knew what a labor organization was supposed to advocate: "It is the industrial, not the race, question we endeavor to solve."[226] The Knights of Labor fought for labor, not racial progress; it was a labor organization, not a racial organization. With the challenge of interracial unionism, however, it was forced to recognize black laborers as equal to white laborers in order to increase the solidarity and power of labor as a

---

[226] *Ibid.*

whole. It was not "so brilliantly egalitarian at its height," as David Roediger believed.[227] Outside of the interests of the labor movement, the Knights of Labor, as an organization, did not care about the equality of blacks to whites. It was a labor organization.[228]

What caused this uproar was not what the Order promoted in its fight for labor, but rather the specter of social equality. The historian Jane Dailey claimed that the Knights of Labor was among the groups (along with Republicans and Populists) that gave black and white Virginians "common political cause" in the late nineteenth century. Therefore, she argued, "The task for the Democrats in Virginia as elsewhere in the late-nineteenth-

---

[227] David R. Roediger, *Towards the Abolition of Whiteness: Essays on Race, Politics, and Working Class History* (New York, 1994) 9.

[228] As it turned out, the Knights of Labor had reached its peak. Within the next decade, the organization was plagued by unsuccessful strikes. Divisions between the skilled laborers and the industrial laborers also hurt the organization. Mismanagement compounded its problems even further. The membership of seven-hundred-thousand in 1886 had dwindled to one-hundred-thousand in 1890, and by 1900 it was practically did not exist. Samuel Gompers had founded a new labor organization called the American Federation of Labor, and it was quickly rising as the premier labor organization in the country – without black membership.

century South was to constrain this coalition and with it the possibility for progressive politics in the South."[229] But in reality, the Democrats did not need to do much work against the Knights, as the fear of social equality (both the term and the vague concept) played its role in hurting what Dailey believes to be an interracial coalition for progressive politics. The incidents surrounding the Richmond convention of the Knights demonstrated that the real issue was so-called social equality, not the Democrats.

Therein lay the challenge of interracial unionism in the South: the bugaboo of social equality. George Washington Cable explained the dilemma much like Powderly might have, "Race fusion is not essential to National unity; such unity requires only civil and political, not private social, homogeneity."[230] He pointed out that others indeed understood his point, "They see that public society comprises all those relations that are impersonal, unselective, and in which all men, of whatever personal inequality, should stand equal. They recognize that

[229] Jane Dailey, *Before Jim Crow: The Politics of Race in Postemanciptaion Virginia* (Chapel Hill, 2000) 14.
[230] Cable, *The Negro Question*, 46.

private society is its opposite hemisphere; that it is personal, selective, assertive, ignores civil equality without violating it, and forms itself entirely upon mutual private preferences and affinities. They agree that civil status has of right no special value in private society, and that their private social status has rightly no special value in their public social – *i.e.*, their merely civil – relations."[231] The trouble though was that so many white Southerners did not agree. In a time of decreasing opportunities for black people in the South, and with the rise of segregation in custom, fears of social equality loomed large – as Powderly found out despite his acquiescent intentions to the South's racial customs.[232] It wasn't as McLaurin thought, "The national leadership of the Knights espoused racial policies decidedly more liberal than those accepted by white southerners."[233] Rather, Powderly was just an

---

[231] *Ibid.*, 44.

[232] For an account of the increasingly tense race relations in the South during this period, see: Rabinowitz, *Race Relations in the Urban South*; Joel Williamson, *The Crucible of Race: Black-White Relations in the American South Since Emancipation* (New York, 1984); Williamson, *A Rage for Order: Black/White Relations in the American South Since Emancipation* (New York, 1986).

[233] McLaurin, *The Knights of Labor in the South*, 132.

example of one of Cable's "Northern minds [that] are often puzzled" at the confusion.[234]

With the blurry lines that Cable described most white Southerners held between any sort of equality and social equality, one finds it hard to imagine, even if industrial equality had been achieved as many white Southerners in the Order believed it should (before the Richmond convention), that these same people would accept equal black workers having similar purchasing power without causing a racket about social equality. Thus, the challenge the Knights of Labor faced posed quite the formidable task indeed – despite its best efforts to remain strictly a labor union that wished to include all workers regardless of any number of social divides such as race or religion. But "social equality" helped overpower the Order's goals.

---

[234] Cable, *The Negro Question*, 44.

Freedom on Behalf of God

Justifying "An Act for Establishing Religious Freedom" in the Newly Independent Commonwealth of Virginia

The first statute in the newly independent United States to establish religious freedom justified the act by opening, "Whereas, Almighty God hath created the mind free." This document, hailed as the beginning of religious freedom in the new nation of liberty and reason, actually reasoned in the name of God. It broke free from religion – by using religion. In hindsight, from the perspective of secular scholars of the twentieth century and beyond, this bill might seem, in a sense, a denunciation of Christianity. It may appear a step in the story of the progress of the United States. Yet, this document embraced Christianity, and argued on behalf of God.[235]

Too often, scholars focus on the essence of this statute for religious freedom from the perspective of the person who drafted it: Thomas Jefferson. Particularly inclined to apply this method are Jefferson's biographers. While on the one hand, such a mode of analysis may seem to make sense, it is misleading. Jefferson was one of the least Christian of the prominent founders. A man devoted to science and the reason of the Enlightenment, he believed three quarters of the Bible was unimportant.

---

[235] Record of the General Assembly, Enrolled Bills, Record Group 78, Library of Virginia.

To understand the bill from his perspective is to perhaps recognize why he drafted it, but it is not to understand why it passed. When the bill finally passed several years after he had first introduced it to the Virginia legislature, Jefferson was not even present for the debate – he was in France. The arguments that convinced legislators to vote for his statute in 1785 were not made strictly on reason as Jefferson might have seen it, but rather these justifications for the bill relied on an embrace of what they believed to be the purest Christian beliefs and behaviors.[236]

When understanding these Christian arguments for religious liberty, it becomes apparent that the support for it was not a step in modernity. Scholars often understand this revolutionary bill to mark the rise of a secular United States – but to view it this way is to view it anachronistically through today's eyes and to make the

---

[236] For biographies of Thomas Jefferson, see: Dumas Malone, *Jefferson and His Time*, 6 vols. (Boston, 1948-1981); Merrill Peterson, *Thomas Jefferson and the New Nation* (New York, 1970); Noble Cunningham, *In Pursuit of Reason: The Life of Thomas Jefferson* (Baton Rouge, 1987); Thomas Jefferson, *The Apostle of Americanism* (Ann Arbor, 1939).

historical reality fit a neat pathway toward what we know today. Moreover, the very degree of radicalism of this bill can be called into question when one realizes that the arguments for religious freedom relied not just on an ideology but also for a desire of social order – the two, contrary to popular perception, were not mutually exclusive. Finally, if one assumes the rise of secular thought and reasoning to be a part of the modernization process, then certainly this statue for religious freedom was not in any way modern. The reason for this is clear: the Western arguments for religious liberty as well as the bill in Virginia embraced Christianity rather than moving away from it.[237]

The argument for this brand of religious freedom came from the political philosopher John Locke, particularly his 1689 published letter on religious

---

[237] For examples of perspectives on religious freedom as a part of increased modernity, progress, and/or secularization, see: Jon Butler, *Becoming America: The Revolution before 1776* (Cambridge, 2000); Chris Beneke, *Beyond Toleration: The Religious Origins of American Pluralism* (New York, 2006); Alan Heimert, *Religion and the American Mind, from the Great Awakening to the Revolution* (Cambridge, 1966).

toleration. His line of reasoning influenced pamphleteers, legislators, and petitioners – all sources this essay will draw upon. Though in 1776 the call for disassociating with the Anglican Church was primarily a patriotic impulse, once Virginia won its independence, the contention shifted toward religious freedom. And they did so by invoking God.

John Locke on Religious Toleration

"Toleration," declared Locke, was "the chief characteristic of the true church." Boasting of one's orthodoxy over those of others "are much rather marks of men's striving for power and empire over one another, than of the church of Christ." As Locke affirmed, "Let anyone have ever so true a claim to all these things, yet if he be destitute of charity, meekness, and goodwill in general towards all mankind, even to those that are not Christians, he is certainly yet short of becoming a true Christian himself." Locke did not denounce what he believed to be true religion; he embraced Christianity by challenging his contemporaries to act like true Christians.[238]

---

[238] John Locke, "A Letter Concerning Toleration," ed. Paul Sigmund, *The Selected Political Writings of John Locke* (New York, 2005), 126.

Locke still supported spreading Christianity, and he believed toleration allowed for the best chance of gaining true converts. By acting un-Christian through boast or force, an individual seemed "careless about his own salvation." Thus, Locke found it difficult "to persuade me that he were extremely concerned for mine [salvation]." As he reasoned, "It is impossible that those should sincerely and heartily apply themselves to make other people Christians, who have not really embraced the Christian religion in their own hearts." Locke argued not against Christianity, but for the sake of the purity of the religion itself: "Whosoever, therefore, is sincerely solicitous about the kingdom of God, and thinks it is his duty to endeavor the enlargement of it amongst men, ought to apply himself with no less care and industry to the rooting out of these immoralities, than to the extirpation of sects."[239]

Anybody who did not practice this type of unadulterated Christianity followed worldly desires, according to Locke. Not practicing toleration was "unbecoming the name of a Christian." One must not act

[239] Locke, "Toleration," ed. Sigmund, *Selected Political Writings*, 127, 128.

"cruel and implacable towards those that differ from him in opinion." If one indeed conducted oneself in such manner, "He plainly demonstrates by his actions, that it is another kingdom he aims at, and not the advancement of the kingdom of God." Locke disapproved of those who "pretend" to act on "a principle of charity" and a "love to men's souls," and who used this façade as reason to "deprive them of their estates, maim them with corporal punishments, starve and torment them in noisome prisons, and in the end even take away their lives." Such behavior was not that of real Christians. Locke cared about promoting pure Christianity.[240]

Using force to establish Christianity was futile in gaining true converts, explained Locke. Compelling people via "fire and sword" to "conform to this or that exterior worship, without any regard had unto their morals" and to force them to "profess things they do not believe" did not "compose a truly Christian church" – to believe that it did was "altogether incredible." Those truly concerned with "our salvation" must "follow the perfect example of that Prince of Peace" in gaining people to Christianity

---

[240] Locke, "Toleration," ed. Sigmund, *Selected Political Writings*, 128, 127.

"prepared with the Gospel of peace, and with exemplary holiness of their conversation [*conduct*]" Thus, Locke wished to carry a pure Christianity by both converter and convert.[241]

He then offered his solution. He wanted to eliminate the conflict between "those that have, or at least pretend to have, on the one side, a concernment for the interest of men's souls, and, on the other side, a care of the commonwealth." Worried about the possibility of "pretenses of loyalty and obedience to the prince, or of tenderness and sincerity in the worship of God," Locke declared, "I esteem it above all things necessary to distinguish *exactly* the business of civil government from that of religion, and to settle the *just* bounds that lie between the one and the other." According to Locke, then, what was the civil government's role in religion?[242]

---

[241] Locke, "Toleration," ed. Sigmund, *Selected Political Writings*, 128, 129. Italics and brackets are not added by the author, but rather can be found in the Norton edition.

[242] Locke, "Toleration," ed. Sigmund, *Selected Political Writings*, 129. Italics and bold are not added by the author, but rather can be found in the Norton edition.

Locke first had to define the civil interest, so he could distinguish it from religion. As he stated, "Civil interest I call life, liberty, health, and indolency of body; and the possession of outward things, such as money, lands, *houses*, furniture, and the like." With this in mind, he could explain the duty of the civil magistrate: "By the impartial execution of equal laws, *by-laws imposed equally on all* to secure unto all the people in general, and to every one of his subjects in particular, the just possession of these things belonging to this life." It was clear to Locke that "the jurisdiction of the magistrate reaches only to these civil concernments."[243]

The magistrate's authority did not extend into the realm of religion. His power "neither can nor ought in any manner to be extended to the salvation of souls." Locke gave three major reasons for this. First, "the care of souls is not committed to the civil magistrate, any more than to other men." The way Locke saw it, "it appears not that God has ever given any such authority to one man over another, as to compel anyone to his religion." Second, the civil magistrate's "power consists only in outward force:

---

[243] Locke, "Toleration," ed. Sigmund, *Selected Political Writings*, 129, 130.

but true and saving religion consists in the inward persuasion of the mind, without which nothing can be acceptable to God." Punishment could not have any "such efficacy as to make men change the inward judgment that they have framed of things." In other words, it was futile to even try. For salvation to work, the faith must "be thoroughly believed by those that so profess and practice." Finally, each person had a right to choose his faith, but even this has strong Christian justification by Locke. As he pointed out, "There being but one truth, one way to heaven; what hopes is there that more men would be led into it, if they had no other rule to follow but the religion of the court [*the prince*] and were put under the necessity to quit [*the light of*] their own reason and [*to oppose,*] the dictates of their own consciences, and blindly to resign up themselves to the will of their governor [the prince], and to the religion which either ignorance, ambition, or superstition had chance to establish[*ed*] in the countries where they were born?" Nonsense, thought Locke.[244]

---

[244] Locke, "Toleration," ed. Sigmund, *Selected Political Writings*, 130, 131, 131-132. Italics, brackets, and bold are not added by the author, but rather can be found in the Norton edition.

"Nobody is born a member of any church," Locke maintained, because a church was "a free and voluntary society." In such a voluntary "religious society" as a church, "nothing ought, nor can be transacted in this society, relating to the possession of civil and worldly goods." Locke was clear in his distinction between religious and civil authority. Referring to the religious society, he claimed, "No force is here to be made use of, upon any occasion whatsoever: for force belongs wholly to the civil magistrate, and the possession of all outward goods is subject to his jurisdiction." By restricting religious activity to a body without jurisdiction force (the church) while at the same time restricting force to a body without jurisdiction over religious activity, Locke separated religion and force from each other – thereby allowing for toleration.[245]

With toleration, came multiple churches, and thus Locke prescribed to them "the duty of toleration" consisting of three parts. First, there was no obligation by any church "to retain any such person in her bosom, as after admonition continues obstinately to offend against

---

[245] Locke, "Toleration," ed. Sigmund, *Selected Political Writings*, 132, 134.

the laws of the [religious] society." Excommunication did not allow for the church to deprive that person of "civil goods," which fell under the power only of the civil magistrate. Rather, excommunication meant simply "that the resolution of the [religious] society in that respect being declared, the union that was between the body and some member, comes thereby to be dissolved." This understanding of the bond between an individual and religious society was similar to his understanding of the same between an individual and civil society.[246]

Second, the duty of toleration required that "no private person has any right in any manner to prejudice another person in his civil enjoyments, because he is of another church or religion... whether he be Christian or pagan." And with various churches coexisting in the same civil society, the duty also required that the principle "concerning the mutual toleration of private persons differing from one another in religion, I understand also of

---

[246] Locke, "Toleration," ed. Sigmund, *Selected Political Writings*, 135. For more on Locke's understanding between an individual and civil society, see: Locke, "The Second Treatise of Government," ed. Sigmund, *Selected Political Writings*, 17-125.

particular churches; which stand as it were in the same relation to each other as private persons among themselves." As he explicitly proclaimed, "Nobody therefore, in fine, neither single persons, nor churches, nay, not even commonwealths, have any just title to invade the civil rights and worldly goods of each other, upon the pretence of religion." Locke was adamant about keeping the religious and civil establishments separate.[247]

Third, Locke placed responsibilities upon those that held ecclesiastical authority. Their influence must not "in any manner be extended to civil affairs." Locke made it clear, "The church itself is a thing absolutely separate and distinct from the commonwealth." Moreover, not only did they have to "abstain from violence and rapine, and all manner of persecution," but they were "obliged also to admonish his hearers of the duties of peace and good-will towards those that differ from them in faith and worship." Locke's ideology thus led to peace, stability, and order – ideology and social order were not mutually exclusive. And still, with his emphasis on Christian peace

---

[247] Locke, "Toleration," ed. Sigmund, *Selected Political Writings*, 135, 135-136, 137-138.

(a la Prince of Peace) and good will, Locke once again used a religious belief to justify the freedom of religion.[248]

Patriotic Support for Religious Liberty

When Virginia, along with twelve other colonies in North America, declared itself independent from the British Empire, sentiment against the Church of England exploded. Such a movement was not only supported by dissenters such as Baptists, but also by former Anglicans who believed they were acting as patriotic citizens of Virginia who wished to sever ties with the church of their enemy. Hence, in a commonwealth whose citizens were particularly supportive of independence, both in numbers and in zeal, the espousal for religious liberty quickly grew. In October of 1776, the legislature of Virginia received a petition signed by ten-thousand citizens of Virginia calling for freedom not only from the Anglican Church but also for a broader religious liberty that allowed for the equal recognition of all religions found in the commonwealth.

The petitioners justified their position in part by claiming it to be the patriotic way. As they declared, "your

---

[248] Locke, "Toleration," ed. Sigmund, *Selected Political Writings*, 138.

petitioners being (in common with the other inhabitants of this commonwealth) delivered from British oppression rejoice in the prospect of having their freedom secured and maintained to them and their posterity individuals." Their patriotic tone continued, "your petitioners therefore having long groaned under the burden of an ecclesiastical establishment beg leave to move your honourable house that this as well as every other yolk may be broken and that the oppressed may go free that so every religious denominations being on a level animosities may cease and that Christian forbearance, grace, and charity, may be practiced toward each other, while the legislature interferes only to support them in their just rights and equal privileges." Even with its appeals to patriotism, the petition still embraced Christianity to argue for justifying religious freedom – just like Locke had done. Moreover, they called for "Equal Liberty! That valuable blessing which though it be the birthright of every good member of the State, is what [torn piece] have been deprived of" through taxation for the church. They invoked, too, an understanding of natural rights, which came from Locke's natural rights, which was itself based on an acceptance of the Creator.[249]

Also writing as the War for Independence continued, "A Freeman of Virginia" presented an argument in favor of religious liberty through a pamphlet in 1776. He hoped his comments in response to a previously published pamphlet that supported an established church in any state would "be of some service to my country." Like the petition, an important part of his plea was patriotic. As he warned, "America is now threatened with every kind of slavery: Is doomed both to civil and religious bondage at once." In fighting the tyranny, the author contended, "Surely we ought at present, if ever, to be joined together in the same mind, and in the same judgment; but as yet, it is not so with us: We are unhapily divided in several respects. – In Virginia, we greatly differ about the worship of GOD." The British enemy was enough of a fight, he thought, "When by GOD's blessing on our endeavours, we have vanquished the common enemy, and have driven the disturbers of our peace, and destroyers of our country, from our

---

[249] Petition, American Memory collection, Library of Congress, http://memory.loc.gov. For more on Locke's pervasive influence in America, see: Jerome Huyler, *Locke in America: The Moral Philosophy of the Founding Era* (Lawrence, 1995).

coasts, we must afterward, many of us, be enslaved as to our better part, our souls, and be forced to yield to the heaviest yoke of oppression? Heaven forbid it!" His call for patriotism was clear, "We are bravely striving to maintain our freedom." He beseeched, "Every sword that is drawn, ever rifle that is fired, every canon that roars, every drop of blood that has been shed in America for some years past, cries, – cries with a loud alarming heart-affecting voice, – *Let there be no ecclesiastical establishment*."[250]

That powerful call, though, was not only on a patriotic basis – it had practical as well as philosophical justifications. The "Freeman" contested the previous pamphlet's assertion that the state could not stand without an established Church. If such was the case, "In vain then is our declaration of Independence." He asked rhetorically, "Are not the Magistrates of every State armed with the legal sword?" If peace and order were the

---

[250] "A Freeman of Virginia," *The Freeman's Remonstrance against an Ecclesiastical Establishment: Being Some Remarks on a Late Pamphlet Entitled the Necessity of an Established Church in Any State* (Williamsburg, 1777), 4, 3, 13. Italics are present in the original text.

concern, then there was no need to worry, even without an established church: "Surely then they have sufficient power to suppress any riot, or tumult, or insurrection that may happen among the subjects of every sect or party."[251] As Locke had suggested, the ideology of religious liberty did not hinder social order.

In fact, just like Locke, the "Freeman" argued that religious liberty helped further secure society's peace and stability. As the "Freeman" pointed out, "When every society of Christians is allowed full, equal, and impartial liberty, what can they desire more? – What advantage could they expect by a revolution, when every one enjoys all the privileges he can wish for already? There can be no danger of mens growing uneasy under such an auspicious government." Such was Locke's recommendation to magistrates, "Let those dissenters enjoy but the same privileges in **civils** [*civil affairs*] as his other subject, and he will quickly find that these religious meetings will be no longer be dangerous."[252] These advocates for religious

---

[251] "Freeman," *Freeman's Remonstrance*, 4.
[252] "Freeman," *Freeman's Remonstrance*, 5; Locke, "Toleration," ed. Sigmund, *Selected Political Writings*, 159. Italics, brackets, and bold are not added by the author, but rather can be found in the

liberty viewed their ideology as a way to support social stability.

Failure to adhere to this ideology posed great risks. The "Freeman" cautioned that when a particular sect of Christianity "is by law exalted to dominion above the rest, this lays the foundation of envy, and debate, and emulation, and wrath, and discord, and confusion; if not war, bloodshed, and slaughter, in the end." Similarly, Locke had declared, "Oppression raises ferments, and makes men struggle to cast off an uneasy tyrannical yoke." As Locke had maintained, "If men enter into seditious conspiracies, it is not religion that inspires them to it in their meetings, but their sufferings and oppressions that make them willing to ease themselves." Religious freedom, according to this argument, indeed held a fear of revolution as well – a point that presumably was not lost on many of the Virginia legislature who later shifted support toward Jefferson's bill.[253]

Norton edition.
[253] "Freeman," *Freeman's Remonstrance*, 5; Locke, "Toleration," ed. Sigmund, *Selected Political Writings*, 160, 159. Bold is not added by the author, but rather can be found in the Norton edition.

The importance of the public good stood prominently in the arguments made by the "Freeman." In response to the previous pamphleteer's accusation that even the signers of the petitions for religious liberty would impose their own churches if they could, the "Freeman" ensured, "We signed the petitions, out of an honest zeal for the public good." In a sense, this was the simultaneously selfless and selfish thing, "We have so often read, and heard, and seen, the baleful consequences of such establishments, that we are really sick of the notion. Nay some of us have long eaten of these sour grapes, and our teeth are set on edge, and now we have no more stomach to such fruit." To him, individual liberty and the public good were mutually dependent.[254]

However, as pragmatic as the "Freeman" sounded in some of his arguments, he also demonstrated his deep philosophical convictions at other points. The issue he had with an established state church was not necessarily the small amount of tribute a citizen would have to pay, but rather it was the mere principle of doing

---

[254] "Freeman," *Freeman's Remonstrance*, 8, 9, 8.

so. As he proclaimed, "A shilling or two is too much to give for nothing. For nothing, did I say!" He likened it to the colonial opposition against the British tax on tea of 1773, "Like the threepenny act on tea, though a trifle in itself, it is a badge of slavery. The worst kind of slavery, SPIRITUAL SLAVERY." The contestation that the "Freeman" held against any sort of religious tax was not the amount of money, nor even the financial burden on a citizen. Rather, he strongly believed that "free men" must not pay such a duty on the basic principle that they were indeed free.[255]

His own position was the most rational position, the "Freeman" insisted. Those who opposed his stance not so, "For what reason can be given, why one society of Christians should be raised to domination over all the rest, many of whom at least, to all appearance, are as pious men, and as good subjects as themselves?" Such an elevation "can never be reconciled to reason; nor even to the common feelings of humanity." Reason and faith did not conflict.[256]

---

[255] "Freeman," *Freeman's Remonstrance*, 11.
[256] "Freeman," *Freeman's Remonstrance*, 10.

When listing his reasons for rejecting the union of "the Christian Church" to "any State whatever," the "Freeman" based his top three choices on the importance and purity of Christianity. First, "The consent of the great PARENT has not been obtained; I mean the Supreme Being." Like Locke, he invoked God to justify the division of the church from the state. He continued, "God is the father of the world by creation, and of the Church by regeneration." Clearly, he held the Protestant belief in the church not being the direct route to God.[257]

In addition, the "Freeman" argued, God rejected such a union of the church and the state. As he pointed out, "There is no ordinance of GOD for this match, nor any person, or persons, appointed by him, to celebrate it. Nay, it is quite contrary to the New Testament. My kingdom is not of this world says our Lord." Just like Locke, he used Christianity to argue against the establishment of a Christian church by the state. Similarly, like Locke, he pointed out that the dominion of this world was not the same as that of God. Thus, no prince could

---

[257] "Freeman," *Freeman's Remonstrance*, 6.

conquer worldly prizes in hopes of expanding God's kingdom.[258]

To do so was to corrupt Christianity – just as Locke espoused. Such a union between the church and the state was unjust because of the "iniquilaty between the parties" that were "very different in characters." As the "Freeman" claimed, "The world is altogether carnal; the Church is made partaker of a divine nature." The Church was too pure to be corrupted by the state, "they are no ways suitable companions." In this way, despite his patriotic appeals, the main thrust of his argument for religious liberty was by a reverence for the Christian God.[259]

Reaction against Religious Assessment Bill of 1784

In 1784, the Virginia legislature considered the passage of "A Bill Establishing a Provision for Teachers of the Christian Religion,"[260] but decided to wait until the following year for a final vote to hear the voice of what their constituents supported. Although the bill allowed

---

[258] "Freeman," *Freeman's Remonstrance*, 6.
[259] "Freeman," *Freeman's Remonstrance*, 7.
[260] Full text can be found in Appendix.

each person to decide to which church he would contribute (a person could donate to education if they chose not to do so to a particular church), a public uproar ensued. Although James Madison initially opposed public commentary on this religious assessment bill, George Nicholas convinced him to encourage citizens of counties to voice their concerns. As Nicholas argued to Madison, "A majority of the counties are in favor of the measure but... a great majority of the people are against it; but if this majority should not appear by petition the fact will be denied." As a response Madison composed the "Memorial and Remonstrance Against Religious Assessments" to help solicit such petitions. The arguments he employed clearly invoked Locke.[261]

Madison's public commentary indeed helped rouse a reaction rejecting the assessment bill. In fact, about one-hundred petitions from almost every county in Virginia flooded the state legislature in its 1785 session in

---

[261] George Nicholas, quoted, Thomas Buckley, *Church and State in Revolutionary Virginia, 1776-1787* (Charlottesville, 1977), 131. Full text of Madison's "Memorial and Remonstrance Against Religious Assessments" can be found in the Appendix.

the fall, with almost all of them opposing the bill. Despite the assessment bill's apparent liberality in allowing a citizen to make the choice of which church (or education) he would support with his payment, the petitioning citizens still overwhelmingly called for further religious liberty: disassociating any established church from the state – precisely the separation of civil and religious societies that Locke had espoused.[262]

However, although Madison's blueprint had success and there were some other petitions from dissenting religious groups, the highest numbers of petitions fit another formula that spread across part of the commonwealth. These most popular petitions argued for religious liberty primarily on the grounds of promoting a pure Christianity uncorrupted by the state – much like Locke and the pamphleteer "Freeman." As one petition announced, "Your petitioners do therefore declare most earnestly declare against it [the assessment bill], believing it to be contrary to the Spirit of the Gospel, and the Bill of

---

[262] According to Buckley, the total number of signatures who opposed the bill outnumbered the number who supported it by a ratio of twelve to one. Buckley, *Church and State in Revolutionary Virginia*, 147.

Rights [of Virginia]." In other words, this petition called upon the legislature to act in what its signers believed to be a more Christian manner. As the petition pointed out, "The blessed Author of our Religion not only maintained and supported his Gospel in the world for several hundred years without Aid of Civil Power, But against all the Powers of the Earth." State sponsorship would not help the clergy, in fact, "on the contrary it might call in many Hirelings, whose chief [illegible word] and desire would be Temporal Interest." The petition's concern was indeed to keep the church pure.[263]

Compulsion by the state to join the church did not increase the dominion of veritable Christianity. As one petition claimed, "The faithful Ministers of the different denominations, who have a real zeal for the welfare of mankind, are contented with the free-will offerings of the People; and none but the Ambitious, the lazy, the luxurious who labour (if it can be called Labour) merely for Gold and not for the God of their Fellow-creatures have need of compulsive Measures for their support."

---

[263] Petition from Goochland County, 2 November 1785, American Memory collection, Library of Congress, http://memory.loc.gov

Like Locke, this petition expressed the corruption of a church influenced by the state, and how such a church could not be truly Christian if it was not supported by voluntary decisions by each individual involved in the religious society. And as Locke had made clear, forced outward behavior to worship a particular religion did not gain any converts because true salvation had to come from the soul. Similarly, a petition argued, "Civil Government are, and ought to be, Independent of Each other... the one has for its object the proper Regulation of the External conduct of men towards each other... the latter has for its object internal and spiritual welfare and is beyond the reach of human laws." As in Locke's philosophy, this petition recognized a difference between the external and the internal.[264]

As Locke had believed, these civil governments were below the laws of God. As one petition explained, "Our Representatives We consider as only vested with a

---

[264] Petition from Fauquier County, 29 November 1785, American Memory collection, Library of Congress, http://memory.loc.gov; Petition from Botetourt County, 29 November 1785, American Memory collection, Library of Congress, http://memory.loc.gov.

Delegated power for the purpose of making such laws as king to promote the happiness of Society." Religion, in its purity, must remain "wholly Distinct from the Secular affairs of Public Society." Moreover, as Locke had described, laws of external worship did not convert people to the true Church because of the lack of conviction as well as the violation of God's will by the magistrate. As a petition argued, "Religion is a personal privilege" and the legislature must not take away "the highest blessing Heaven affords us" by attempting to "control us in that most valuable birthright!" The petitions faith in the strength of Christianity continued, "How can we doubt of the existence of Christianity?" Christianity was "superior to and independent upon all civil all civil laws." The freedom of religion from the state was crucial precisely because the faith's law was above the state's law because it was too divine and pure to be regulated by the worldly government.[265]

---

[265] Petition from Rockbridge County, 2 November 1785, American Memory collection, Library of Congress, http://memory.loc.gov; Petition from Washington County, 10 December 1785, American Memory collection, Library of Congress, http://memory.loc.gov.

"An Act for Establishing Religious Freedom"[266]

With almost one-hundred petitions submitted to Virginia's legislature during its session in fall 1785, and most of them favoring religious freedom, the legislature responded. Jefferson was in France, but Madison was there to introduce again the bill Jefferson had drafted in 1777. "An Act for establishing religious Freedom" passed, to take effect beginning in 1786. But what did this law say? More specifically, how did this law justify the establishment of religious freedom?

It began by invoking Locke's God: "Whereas, Almighty God hath created the mind free." It continued in that vein, "All attempts to influence it by temporal punishments or burthens, or by civil incapacitations tend only to beget habits of hypocrisy and meanness, and are a departure from the plan of the holy author of our religion." As Locke had stated, such attempts made the so-called Christian behave unlike a good Christian, thus the converter became a hypocrite. The Lord "both of body and mind yet chose not to propagate it by coercions on either, as was in his Almighty power to do." Christianity

---

[266] Full text can be found in Appendix.

emphasized peace, as Locke had highlighted repeatedly. In this way, the statute of religious freedom emphasized the importance of acting like true Christians.[267]

As the bill's argument continued, the focus shifted to the corruptibility of rulers, like Locke had contended. "The impious presumption of legislators and rulers, civil as well as ecclesiastical, who, being themselves but fallible and uninspired men have assumed dominion over the faith of others, setting up their own opinions and modes of thinking as the only true and infallible, and as such endeavouring to impose them on others, hath established and maintained false religions over the greatest part of the world and through all time." This recognition of rulers as mortals and no more knowing about religion than any other man came from Locke. As he has argued, "Neither the right, nor the art of ruling, does necessarily carry along with it the certain knowledge of other things; and least of all of the true religion." If any a prince truly understood the way to salvation, then Locke asked, "How could it come to pass that the lords of the earth should differ so vastly as they do in religious

---

[267] For quotations from the bill for religious freedom, see appendix.

matters?" Like Locke, the bill pointed out the different religions forced by rulers in history, and used that to strengthen the point of the false religions espoused by these rulers. Locke had emphasized, "The one only narrow way which leads to heaven is not better known to the magistrate than to private persons, and therefore I cannot safely take him for my guide, who may probably be as ignorant of the way as myself, and who certainly is less concerned for my salvation than I myself am." This lack of faith in the ruler's beliefs by Locke clearly manifested itself in the Virginia statute – and once again, the end goal was salvation by the true means.[268]

The statute, like Locke, emphasized the right of each man to choose for himself what religious society he joins. The statute disapproved of any other course: "Even the forcing him to support this or that teacher of his own religious persuasion is depriving him of the comfortable liberty of giving his contributions to the particular pastor, whose morals he would make his pattern, and whose powers he feels most persuasive to righteousness." Locke

---

[268] For quotations from the bill for religious freedom, see appendix; Locke, "Toleration," ed. Sigmund, *Selected Political Writings*, 141, 142.

had extensively discussed the importance of religious societies being voluntary. Furthermore, as Locke had declared, "liberty of conscience is every man's natural right." The statute certainly recognized that right. That persuasion of conscience was the key. Even if the civil magistrate happened to impose the right religion, "yet if I be not thoroughly persuaded thereof in my own mind, there will be no safety for me in following it. No way whatsoever that I shall walk in against the dictates of my conscience, will ever bring me to the mansions of the blessed." In fact, such requisites were not only a violation of natural rights, but also futile to the Christian cause of saving souls. Locke articulated, "Whatsoever is not done with that assurance of faith, is neither well in itself, nor can it be acceptable to God." He explained, "In vain, therefore, do princes compel their subjects to come into their church-communion, under pretence of saving their souls." Such behavior only perverted the Church and its practices. As he maintained, "To impose such things, therefore, upon any people, contrary to their own judgment, is, in effect, to command them to offend God." Locke had reasoned as a Christian, as did the bill.[269]

---

[269] For quotations from the bill for religious freedom,

As Locke had described, the church and the civil magistrate had to remain separate. Therefore, their respective punishments could not overlap. Hence, as the statute stated, "to suffer the civil magistrate to intrude his powers into the field of opinion and to restrain the profession or propagation of principles on supposition of their ill tendency is a dangerous fallacy which at once destroys all religious liberty because he being of course judge of that tendency will make his opinions the rule of judgment and approve or condemn the sentiments of others only as they shall square with or differ from his own." John Locke had pointed to the rights of people to hold opinions, devoid of the civil magistrate's influence. He had claimed, "Speculative opinions, therefore, and articles of faith, as they are called, which are required only to be believed, cannot be imposed on any church by the law of the land." Moreover, he contended, "The business of laws is not to provide for the truth of opinions, but for the safety and security of the commonwealth." The statute also stated, "To compel a man to furnish contributions of money for the

---

see appendix; Locke, "Toleration," ed. Sigmund, *Selected Political Writings*, 158, 143, 145, 144, 145.

propagation of opinions which he disbelieves is sinful and tyrannical." Once again, Locke's influence permeated. As Locke had argued, "The magistrate cannot take away these worldly things from this man, or party, and give them to that; nor charge property amongst fellow subjects (*citizens*], no, not even by a law, for a cause that has no relation to the end of civil government." These two realms did not mix, according to both the bill and to Locke. Thus, not just force, but taxation for the church as well did not have any place in this philosophy.[270]

There was no danger, Locke had insisted, in allowing for a society without an established church, even by those who did not follow the right path to salvation. With every man left to care for his own soul, indeed some would neglect to do so. But this did not mandate laws by the magistrate to fix the situation. Locke had drawn an analogy to those who neglect their health or estate to illustrate his point; laws did not "guard them from the negligence or ill husbandry of the possessors themselves."

---

[270] For quotations from the bill for religious freedom, see appendix; Locke, "Toleration," ed. Sigmund, *Selected Political Writings*, 152, 153. 155. Italics, brackets, and bold are not added by the author, but rather can be found in the Norton edition.

Even idolatry should be tolerated, Locke had explained, "because they are not prejudicial to other men's rights, nor do they break the public peace of societies." The key was that religious beliefs "had no manner of relation to the *civil* rights of the subjects." With this understanding, the statute rationalized, "Our civil rights have no dependence on our religious opinions any more than our opinions in physics or geometry, that therefore the proscribing any citizen as unworthy the public confidence, by laying upon him an incapacity of being called to offices of trust and emolument." Clearly, the line of reasoning was parallel.[271]

But as has become evident, these arguments were made as Christians. God ruled above all – not with the civil magistrate, not through the civil magistrate, but above him. The statute declared, "Truth is great, and will prevail if left to herself, that she is the proper and sufficient antagonist to error, and has nothing to fear from the conflict, unless by human interposition disarmed

---

[271] For quotations from the bill for religious freedom, see appendix; Locke, "Toleration," ed. Sigmund, *Selected Political Writings*, 140, 150. 152. Italics are not added by the author, but rather can be found in the Norton edition.

of her natural weapons free argument and debate, errors ceasing to be dangerous when it is permitted freely to contradict them" Similarly, Locke had made clear, "Obedience is due in the first place to God, and afterwards to the laws." As such, both Locke and the statute embraced Christianity to make their case for religious freedom. While today's perspective may make it seem as though the story of the rise of religious liberty is a story of increasing modernization and secularism, of increased rationalization and a rejection of faith, in reality the origins of religious freedom in Virginia, the United States, and the Western tradition rely upon a championing of the purest Christian doctrine.[272]

---

[272] For quotations from the bill for religious freedom, see appendix; Locke, "Toleration," ed. Sigmund, *Selected Political Writings*, 155.

Appendix A

Full Text of "A Bill Establishing a Provision for Teachers of the Christian Religion"[273]

Whereas the general diffusion of Christian knowledge hath a natural tendency to correct the morals of men, restrain their vices, and preserve the peace of society; which cannot be effected without a competent provision for learned teachers, who may be thereby enabled to devote their time and attention to the duty of instructing such citizens, as from their circumstances and want of education, cannot otherwise attain such knowledge; and it is judged that such provision may be made by the Legislature, without counteracting the liberal principle heretofore adopted and intended to be preserved by abolishing all distinctions of pre-eminence amongst the different societies or communities of Christians;

Be it therefore enacted by the General Assembly, That for the support of Christian teachers, _____ per centum on the amount, or _____ in the pound on the sum payable for tax on the property within this Commonwealth, is hereby assessed, and shall be paid by every person chargeable with the said tax at the time the same shall become due; and the Sheriffs of the

---

[273] Thomas Buckley, *Church and State in Revolutionary Virginia, 1776-1787* (Charlottesville, 1977).

several Counties shall have power to levy and collect the same in the same manner and under the like restrictions and limitations, as are or may be prescribed by the laws for raising the Revenues of this State.

And be it enacted, That for every sum so paid, the Sheriff or Collector shall give a receipt, expressing therein to what society of Christians the person from whom he may receive the same shall direct the money to be paid, keeping a distinct account thereof in his books. The Sheriff of every County, shall, on or before the _____ day of _____ in every year, return to the Court, upon oath, two alphabetical lists of the payments to him made. distinguishing in columns opposite to the names of the persons who shall have paid the same, the society to which the money so paid was by them appropriated; and one column for the names where no appropriation shall be made. One of which lists, after being recorded in a book to be kept for that purpose, shall be filed by the Clerk in his office, the other shall by the Sheriff be fixed up in the Court-house, there to remain for the inspection of all concerned. And the Sheriff, after deducting five per centum for the collection, shall forthwith pay to such person or persons as shall be appointed to receive the same by the Vestry, Elders, or Directors, however denominated of each such society, the sum so stated to be due to that society; or in default thereof, upon the motion of such person or persons to the next or any succeeding Court, execution shall be awarded for the same against the Sheriff and his security, his and their executors or administrators; provided that ten days previous notice be give of such motion. And upon every such execution, the Officer serving the same shall proceed to immediate sale of the estate taken, and shall not accept of security for payment at the end of three months, nor to have the goods forthcoming at the day of sale; for his better direction wherein, the Clerk shall endorse upon every such execution that no security of any kind shall be taken.

And be it further enacted, That the money to be raised by virtue of this Act, shall be by the Vestries, Elders, or Directors of each religious society, appropriated to a provision for a Minister or Teacher of the Gospel of their denomination, or the providing places of divine worship, and to none other use whatsoever, except in the denominations of Quakers and Menonists, who may receive what is collected from their members, and place it in their general fund, to be disposed of in a manner which they shall think best calculated to promote their particular mode of worship.

And be it enacted, That all sums which at the time of payment to the Sheriff or Collector may not be appropriated by the person paying the same, shall be accounted for with the Court in manner as by this Act is directed; and after deducting for his collection, the Sheriff shall pay the amount thereof (upon account certified by the Court to the Auditors of Public

Accounts, and by them to the Treasurer) into the public Treasury, to be disposed of under the direction of the General Assembly, for the encouragement of seminaries of learning within the Counties whence such sums shall arise, and to no other use or purpose whatsoever.

THIS Act shall commence, and be in force, from and after the _____ day of _____ in the year _____

John Beckley, C.H.D.

Appendix B

Full Text of James Madison's "Memorial and Remonstrance Against Religious Assessments"[274]

To the Honorable the General Assembly of the Commonwealth of Virginia

A Memorial and Remonstrance Against Religious Assessments

We the subscribers, citizens of the said Commonwealth, having taken into serious consideration, a Bill printed by order of the last Session of General Assembly, entitled "A Bill establishing a provision for Teachers of the Christian Religion," and conceiving that the same if finally armed with the sanctions of a law, will be a dangerous abuse of power, are bound as faithful members of a free State to remonstrate against it, and to declare the reasons by which we are determined. We remonstrate against the said Bill,

1. Because we hold it for a fundamental and undeniable truth, "that religion or the duty which we owe to our Creator and the manner of discharging it, can be directed only by reason and conviction, not by force or violence." The Religion then of every man must be left to the conviction and conscience of every man; and it is the right of every man to

---

[274] Accessed in April 2008 at
http://religiousfreedom.lib.virginia.edu/sacred/madison_m&r_1785.html

exercise it as these may dictate. This right is in its nature an unalienable right. It is unalienable, because the opinions of men, depending only on the evidence contemplated by their own minds cannot follow the dictates of other men: It is unalienable also, because what is here a right towards men, is a duty towards the Creator. It is the duty of every man to render to the Creator such homage and such only as he believes to be acceptable to him. This duty is precedent, both in order of time and in degree of obligation, to the claims of Civil Society. Before any man can be considered as a member of Civil Society, he must be considered as a subject of the Governour of the Universe: And if a member of Civil Society, do it with a saving of his allegiance to the Universal Sovereign. We maintain therefore that in matters of Religion, no man's right is abridged by the institution of Civil Society and that Religion is wholly exempt from its cognizance. True it is, that no other rule exists, by which any question which may divide a Society, can be ultimately determined, but the will of the majority; but it is also true that the majority may trespass on the rights of the minority.

2. Because Religion be exempt from the authority of the Society at large, still less can it be subject to that of the Legislative Body. The latter are but the creatures and vicegerents of the former. Their jurisdiction is both derivative and limited: it is limited with regard to the co-ordinate

169

departments, more necessarily is it limited with regard to the constituents. The preservation of a free Government requires not merely, that the metes and bounds which separate each department of power be invariably maintained; but more especially that neither of them be suffered to overleap the great Barrier which defends the rights of the people. The Rulers who are guilty of such an encroachment, exceed the commission from which they derive their authority, and are Tyrants. The People who submit to it are governed by laws made neither by themselves nor by an authority derived from them, and are slaves.

3. Because it is proper to take alarm at the first experiment on our liberties. We hold this prudent jealousy to be the first duty of Citizens, and one of the noblest characteristics of the late Revolution. The free men of America did not wait till usurped power had strengthened itself by exercise, and entangled the question in precedents. They saw all the consequences in the principle, and they avoided the consequences by denying the principle. We revere this lesson too much soon to forget it. Who does not see that the same authority which can establish Christianity, in exclusion of all other Religions, may establish with the same ease any particular sect of Christians, in exclusion of all other Sects? that the same authority which can force a citizen to contribute three pence only of his property for the support of any one

establishment, may force him to conform to any other establishment in all cases whatsoever?

4. Because the Bill violates the equality which ought to be the basis of every law, and which is more indispensible, in proportion as the validity or expediency of any law is more liable to be impeached. If "all men are by nature equally free and independent," all men are to be considered as entering into Society on equal conditions; as relinquishing no more, and therefore retaining no less, one than another, of their natural rights. Above all are they to be considered as retaining an "equal title to the free exercise of Religion according to the dictates of Conscience." Whilst we assert for ourselves a freedom to embrace, to profess and to observe the Religion which we believe to be of divine origin, we cannot deny an equal freedom to those whose minds have not yet yielded to the evidence which has convinced us. If this freedom be abused, it is an offence against God, not against man: To God, therefore, not to man, must an account of it be rendered. As the Bill violates equality by subjecting some to peculiar burdens, so it violates the same principle, by granting to others peculiar exemptions. Are the Quakers and Menonists the only sects who think a compulsive support of their Religions unnecessary and unwarrantable? can their piety alone be entrusted with the care of public worship? Ought their Religions to be endowed above all others with extraordinary privileges by

which proselytes may be enticed from all others? We think too favorably of the justice and good sense of these denominations to believe that they either covet pre-eminences over their fellow citizens or that they will be seduced by them from the common opposition to the measure.

5. Because the Bill implies either that the Civil Magistrate is a competent Judge of Religious Truth; or that he may employ Religion as an engine of Civil policy. The first is an arrogant pretension falsified by the contradictory opinions of Rulers in all ages, and throughout the world: the second an unhallowed perversion of the means of salvation.

6. Because the establishment proposed by the Bill is not requisite for the support of the Christian Religion. To say that it is, is a contradiction to the Christian Religion itself, for every page of it disavows a dependence on the powers of this world: it is a contradiction to fact; for it is known that this Religion both existed and flourished, not only without the support of human laws, but in spite of every opposition from them, and not only during the period of miraculous aid, but long after it had been left to its own evidence and the ordinary care of Providence. Nay, it is a contradiction in terms; for a Religion not invented by human policy, must have pre-existed and been supported, before it was established by human policy. It is

moreover to weaken in those who profess this Religion a pious confidence in its innate excellence and the patronage of its Author; and to foster in those who still reject it, a suspicion that its friends are too conscious of its fallacies to trust it to its own merits.

7. Because experience witnesseth that ecclesiastical establishments, instead of maintaining the purity and efficacy of Religion, have had a contrary operation. During almost fifteen centuries has the legal establishment of Christianity been on trial. What have been its fruits? More or less in all places, pride and indolence in the Clergy, ignorance and servility in the laity, in both, superstition, bigotry and persecution. Enquire of the Teachers of Christianity for the ages in which it appeared in its greatest lustre; those of every sect, point to the ages prior to its incorporation with Civil policy. Propose a restoration of this primitive State in which its Teachers depended on the voluntary rewards of their flocks, many of them predict its downfall. On which Side ought their testimony to have greatest weight, when for or when against their interest?

8. Because the establishment in question is not necessary for the support of Civil Government. If it be urged as necessary for the support of Civil Government only as it is a means of supporting Religion, and it be not necessary for the latter purpose, it cannot be necessary for the former. If Religion be

not within the cognizance of Civil Government how can its legal establishment be necessary to Civil Government? What influence in fact have ecclesiastical establishments had on Civil Society? In some instances, they have been seen to erect a spiritual tyranny on the ruins of the Civil authority; in many instances they have been seen upholding the thrones of political tyranny: in no instance have they been seen the guardians of the liberties of the people. Rulers who wished to subvert the public liberty, may have found an established Clergy convenient auxiliaries. A just Government instituted to secure & perpetuate it needs them not. Such a Government will be best supported by protecting every Citizen in the enjoyment of his Religion with the same equal hand which protects his person and his property; by neither invading the equal rights of any Sect, nor suffering any Sect to invade those of another.

9. Because the proposed establishment is a departure from the generous policy, which, offering an Asylum to the persecuted and oppressed of every Nation and Religion, promised a lustre to our country, and an accession to the number of its citizens. What a melancholy mark is the Bill of sudden degeneracy? Instead of holding forth an Asylum to the persecuted, it is itself a signal of persecution. It degrades from the equal rank of Citizens all those whose opinions in Religion do not bend to those of the Legislative authority. Distant as it may be in its present form from the Inquisition, it differs from it

only in degree. The one is the first step, the other the last in the career of intolerance. The magnanimous sufferer under this cruel scourge in foreign Regions, must view the Bill as a Beacon on our Coast, warning him to seek some other haven, where liberty and philanthropy in their due extent, may offer a more certain repose from his Troubles.

10. Because it will have a like tendency to banish our Citizens. The allurements presented by other situations are every day thinning their number. To superadd a fresh motive to emigration by revoking the liberty which they now enjoy, would be the same species of folly which has dishonoured and depopulated flourishing kingdoms

11. Because it will destroy that moderation and harmony which the forbearance of our laws to intermeddle with Religion has produced among its several sects. Torrents of blood have been split in the old world, by vain attempts of the secular arm, to extinguish Religious discord, by proscribing all difference in Religious opinion. Time has at length revealed the true remedy. Every relaxation of narrow and rigorous policy, wherever it has been tried, has been found to assuage the disease. The American Theatre has exhibited proofs that equal and compleat liberty, if it does not wholly eradicate it, sufficiently destroys its malignant influence on the health and prosperity of the State. If with the salutary effects of this system under our own eyes, we begin to contract the bounds of Religious freedom, we know no

175

name that will too severely reproach our folly. At least let warning be taken at the first fruits of the threatened innovation. The very appearance of the Bill has transformed "that Christian forbearance, love and charity," which of late mutually prevailed, into animosities and jealousies, which may not soon be appeased. What mischiefs may not be dreaded, should this enemy to the public quiet be armed with the force of a law?

12. Because the policy of the Bill is adverse to the diffusion of the light of Christianity. The first wish of those who enjoy this precious gift ought to be that it may be imparted to the whole race of mankind. Compare the number of those who have as yet received it with the number still remaining under the dominion of false Religions; and how small is the former! Does the policy of the Bill tend to lessen the disproportion? No; it at once discourages those who are strangers to the light of revelation from coming into the Region of it; and countenances by example the nations who continue in darkness, in shutting out those who might convey it to them. Instead of Levelling as far as possible, every obstacle to the victorious progress of Truth, the Bill with an ignoble and unchristian timidity would circumscribe it with a wall of defence against the encroachments of error.

13. Because attempts to enforce by legal sanctions, acts obnoxious to go great a proportion of Citizens, tend to enervate

the laws in general, and to slacken the bands of Society. If it be difficult to execute any law which is not generally deemed necessary or salutary, what must be the case, where it is deemed invalid and dangerous? And what may be the effect of so striking an example of impotency in the Government, on its general authority?

14. Because a measure of such singular magnitude and delicacy ought not to be imposed, without the clearest evidence that it is called for by a majority of citizens, and no satisfactory method is yet proposed by which the voice of the majority in this case may be determined, or its influence secured. The people of the respective counties are indeed requested to signify their opinion respecting the adoption of the Bill to the next Session of Assembly." But the representatives or of the Counties will be that of the people. Our hope is that neither of the former will, after due consideration, espouse the dangerous principle of the Bill. Should the event disappoint us, it will still leave us in full confidence, that a fair appeal to the latter will reverse the sentence against our liberties.

15. Because finally, "the equal right of every citizen to the free exercise of his Religion according to the dictates of conscience" is held by the same tenure with all our other rights. If we recur to its origin, it is equally the gift of nature; if we weigh its importance, it cannot be less dear to us; if we consult

the "Declaration of those rights which pertain to the good people of Virginia, as the basis and foundation of Government," it is enumerated with equal solemnity, or rather studied emphasis. Either the, we must say, that the Will of the Legislature is the only measure of their authority; and that in the plenitude of this authority, they may sweep away all our fundamental rights; or, that they are bound to leave this particular right untouched and sacred: Either we must say, that they may controul the freedom of the press, may abolish the Trial by Jury, may swallow up the Executive and Judiciary Powers of the State; nay that they may despoil us of our very right of suffrage, and erect themselves into an independent and hereditary Assembly or, we must say, that they have no authority to enact into the law the Bill under consideration.

We the Subscribers say, that the General Assembly of this Commonwealth have no such authority: And that no effort may be omitted on our part against so dangerous an usurpation, we oppose to it, this remonstrance; earnestly praying, as we are in duty bound, that the Supreme Lawgiver of the Universe, by illuminating those to whom it is addressed, may on the one hand, turn their Councils from every act which would affront his holy prerogative, or violate the trust committed to them: and on the other, guide them into every measure which may be worthy of his [blessing, may re]dound to their own praise, and may establish more firmly the liberties, the prosperity and the happiness of the Commonwealth.

Appendix C

Full Text of the 1786 Virginia Statute of Religious Freedom[275]

An Act for establishing religious Freedom.

Whereas, Almighty God hath created the mind free; that all attempts to influence it by temporal punishments or burthens, or by civil incapacitations tend only to beget habits of hypocrisy and meanness, and are a departure from the plan of the holy author of our religion, who being Lord, both of body and mind yet chose not to propagate it by coercions on either, as was in his Almighty power to do, that the impious presumption of legislators and rulers, civil as well as ecclesiastical, who, being themselves but fallible and uninspired men have assumed dominion over the faith of others, setting up their own opinions and modes of thinking as the only true and infallible, and as such endeavouring to impose them on others, hath established and maintained false religions over the greatest part of the world and through all time; that to compel a man to furnish contributions of money for the propagation of opinions which he disbelieves is sinful and tyrannical; that even the forcing him to support this or that teacher of his own religious persuasion is depriving him of the comfortable liberty of giving his

---

[275] Record of the General Assembly, Enrolled Bills, Record Group 78, Library of Virginia.

contributions to the particular pastor, whose morals he would make his pattern, and whose powers he feels most persuasive to righteousness, and is withdrawing from the Ministry those temporary rewards, which, proceeding from an approbation of their personal conduct are an additional incitement to earnest and unremitting labours for the instruction of mankind; that our civil rights have no dependence on our religious opinions any more than our opinions in physics or geometry, that therefore the proscribing any citizen as unworthy the public confidence, by laying upon him an incapacity of being called to offices of trust and emolument, unless he profess or renounce this or that religious opinion, is depriving him injuriously of those privileges and advantages, to which, in common with his fellow citizens, he has a natural right, that it tends only to corrupt the principles of that very Religion it is meant to encourage, by bribing with a monopoly of worldly honours and emoluments those who will externally profess and conform to it; that though indeed, these are criminal who do not withstand such temptation, yet neither are those innocent who lay the bait in their way; that to suffer the civil magistrate to intrude his powers into the field of opinion and to restrain the profession or propagation of principles on supposition of their ill tendency is a dangerous fallacy which at once destroys all religious liberty because he being of course judge of that tendency will make his opinions the rule of judgment and approve or condemn the sentiments of others only as they shall square with or differ from his own; that it is time enough for the rightful purposes of civil government, for its officers to interfere when principles break out into overt acts against peace and good order; and finally, that Truth is great, and will prevail if left to herself, that she is the proper and sufficient antagonist to error, and has nothing to fear from the conflict, unless by human interposition disarmed of her natural weapons free argument and debate, errors ceasing to be dangerous when it is permitted freely to contradict them: Be it enacted by General Assembly that no man shall be compelled to frequent or support any religious worship, place, or ministry whatsoever, nor shall be enforced, restrained, molested, or burthened in his body or goods, nor shall otherwise suffer on account of his religious opinions or belief, but that all men shall be free to profess, and by argument to maintain, their opinions in matters of Religion, and that the same shall in no wise diminish, enlarge or affect their civil capacities. And though we well know that this Assembly elected by the people for the ordinary purposes of Legislation only, have no power to restrain the acts of succeeding Assemblies constituted with powers equal to our own, and that therefore to declare this act irrevocable would be of no effect in law; yet we are free to declare, and do declare that the rights hereby asserted, are of the natural rights of mankind, and that if any act shall be hereafter passed to repeal the present or to narrow its operation, such act will be an infringement of natural right.

Exd: ARCHIBALD CARY S.S.

Exd. BENJ HARRISON Sp HD

Afterword

Race and religion in politics has come to a crescendo in the year 2020. First, the COVID-19 pandemic raised questions about racial equality with a disproportionate effect on people of color, both in health and the impact of economic shutdowns. It also raised questions of religious freedom, the role of the state in public health balanced with the freedom to worship together. Second, the murder by a policeman of George Floyd in Minneapolis that thrust (again) the issue of police brutality and its ties to underlying racial inequalities in our society. While this has been ongoing for generations, the recent string of videos has intensified the dialogue, with this particular incident leading to a national and global set of events bringing this issue a renewed awareness and discourse. Finally, the U.S. Presidential election in November 2020 involving one of the most controversial candidates in American history intensifies rhetoric, stakes, and sense of moment.

My aim in this collection of essays has neither been to advocate for a particular set of policy positions, nor do I intend to tell anyone they are right or wrong.

Instead, I hope to have challenged you, the reader, to think more deeply about these issues, with the corresponding complexity each topic deserves, and more importantly, I hope to have challenged your biases. Perhaps you feel more informed about these important moments in American history by reading these essays. I ask that we don't use that knowledge to deride anyone, as this collection reveals no clear "right" position that fits into our political boxes. Let us instead use the thought-provoking insights as a way to inquire further, step back with humility regarding what we think we know, and explore elements of what all of our citizens believe to create integrated solutions applied constructively for our collective good. But first, we must ask more questions.

There is no "right side of history." The assumption of such a trope implies a narrative that sees a march of time toward a predetermined outcome biased to each espouser's notion of progress. When an observer judges history and historical actors based upon his current understanding of progress, he loses sight of the purpose of such work to illuminate his understanding of both past and present. History is stark, layered, bumpy, full of contingencies, and driven by human decisions on scales both micro and macro. Let us exercise these decisions by practicing empiricism over dogmatism, embracing complexity over simplicity, and blurring the lines instead of drawing them.

Raffi E. Andonian

Saint Louis, Missouri

July 2020

Made in the USA
Monee, IL
19 July 2020

36067687R00111